CONSTRUCTION LIKE SUSHI

A fun, handy workbook, reference and study guide for easily undertaking and organizing building construction or improvement projects including a section on almost everything you wanted to know about sushi

By

W. GARY WESTERNOFF
TAEMI WESTERNOFF

Copyright © 2011 by W. Gary Westernoff

Library of Congress Control Number: 2011905672

ISBN 978-0-9668245-1-3

All rights reserved. No part of this work covered by the copyright hereon may be reproduced or used in any form or by any means – graphic, electronic, or mechanical, including photocopying, recording, taping, or storage and retrieval systems – without the written permission of the publisher.

Manufactured in the United States of America

Published by The Westernoff Group
P.O. Box 153
Moraga, CA 94556

Editor: W. Gary Westernoff
Photography: W. Gary Westernoff
Illustration: Miho Owada
Production design: Taemi Westernoff
Sushi preparation: Taemi Westernoff
Worksheets: W. Gary Westernoff

About the Authors

The authors in Japan with friends

W. Gary Westernoff has over thirty years of experience planning, designing and building construction projects throughout the United States and the Pacific Rim as a corporate executive, licensed general contractor, consultant, educator and writer. Inspiration for this book came from users of his web site, www.constructionplace.com, launched in 1999, and the overwhelming demands for more simplicity and transparency in the Construction and Real Estate Industries, his Japan travels, and love of Japanese cuisine. Gary believes that most construction professionals take pride in performing good work in a timely manner, but are sometimes prohibited from doing so because of misunderstandings and poor communication.

Taemi Westernoff was born and raised in Japan. She holds Japan licenses in the traditional Japanese tea ceremony, table coordination, flower arrangement and has over 30 years of international travel and cooking experience. She specializes in preparing fun, easy and healthy dishes including traditional and creative sushi.

DISCLOSURE AND BOOK LIMITATIONS

The information in this book has been gathered from the training and experience of the authors. Neither the authors nor the publisher pretends to offer legal advice or advice on other professional specializations. If such advice is required, it is recommended that the reader obtain it from the properly qualified professional or legal authorities.

DISCLAIMER

The authors and publisher specifically disclaim any liability, loss, or risk, personal or otherwise which is incurred as a consequence directly or indirectly of the use and application of any of the contents of this book.

The Westernoff Group
P.O. Box 153
Moraga, CA 94556
Web site: www.constructionplace.com
E-mail: twg@constructionplace.com

Contents

FORWARD 5

CONSTRUCTION 6

Planning and Resources 9
    PLANNING (1.1) 9
    HIRING PROFESSIONALS (1.2) 18

Costing and Contracting 27
    RFP (Request for Proposal) (2.1) 27
    PROCEDURAL MEMORANDUM (2.2) 34
    PROPOSAL/AGREEMENT (2.3) 41
    TERMS AND CONDITIONS (2.3a) 47
    RFP and PROPOSAL/AGREEMENT Continuation Page (2.4) 47
    COMPARING BIDS (2.5) 50

Work Performance 53
    AGENDA (3.1) 54
    WORK REPORT (3.2) 57
    WORK REPORT Continuation Page (3.3) 57

Making Payments 61
    PAYMENTS AND LIENS 61
    PROGRESS PAYMENTS 62
    FINAL PAYMENT 62

Glossary 69

SUSHI 90

Brief History of Sushi 91

Planning Sushi 92
    Most Common Sushi Ingredients 93
    Utensils for Making Sushi 95

Preparation 99
    Rice 99
    Making Sushi Rice 102
    Chirashi Zushi 103
    Nigiri Zushi 104
    Maki Zushi 106
    Inari Zushi 111
    Oshi Zushi 113

Plating 116

Chop Sticks Manners 116

Bibliography 117

Forward

This book includes two totally unrelated and dissimilar topics. For fun and enjoyment we want to demonstrate that undertaking building construction activities can be easy and fun as making sushi.

Gary Westernoff's first handbook "Construction Management Made Easy" focused on the management process. Whereas, the first (**Construction**) section of this book contains a unique simple four part system designed for the client and/or construction professional because he has discovered that too often steps in the construction management process are duplicated or ignored causing confusion, frustration, poor communication and conflicts, not to mention lots of lost money due to time delays caused by not having a clear meeting of the minds. Also, projects such as home improvements, do not necessarily lend themselves to the entire construction management process. This unique and flexible four part system is designed to work with any type and size of the project including home improvement projects or maintenance repairs.

The second (**Sushi**) section of this book contains a four part overview and systematic approach to understanding and making sushi through pictures and demonstrations. This unique four part overview is written to guide the reader to understand the sushi making process is similar to the construction process. Eventually, we hope the reader can realize that undertaking construction projects can be as fun as making sushi.

Construction

This section of the book includes a unique flexible four part building construction system, number of helpful and productivity tips, and an enhanced version of the Glossary found in the author's earlier publication "Construction Management Made Easy".

Planning and Resources
Costing and Contracting
Work Performance
Making Payments

Each part contains a series of worksheets designed to lead the user through the respective part(s) for use by and for the mutual benefit of the construction professional and the client or property owner. And many of the worksheets have been designed for use as PDF files and are planned for internet use,

Determining what worksheets to use

Commercial or Residential Project Types					
New Construction	Remodel	Home Improvements	Tenant Improvements	Repairs	Maintenance

Worksheets

Use the following tables are for determining the appropriate worksheet(s) to use for your specific project. The number of pages for each worksheet is shown in (parenthesis) after the worksheet description.

Planning and Resources

1.1
Planning (7)

(All projects except Maintenance and Repairs)

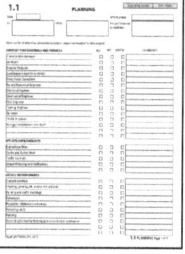

1.2
Hiring Professionals (2)

(All Projects)

Costing and Contracting

2.1 RFP (1)	2.2 Procedural Memorandum (5)	2.3 Proposal Agreement (1)	2.3a Terms and Conditions (1)	2.4 RFP and Proposal Continuation Page (1)	2.5 Comparing Bids (1)
(All Projects)	(All projects except Maintenance and Repairs)	(All Projects)	(All Projects)	(If necessary)	(All Projects)
	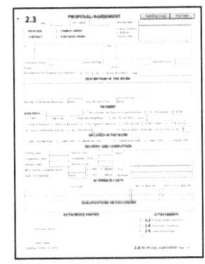	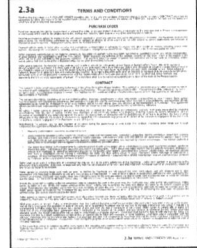			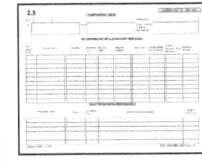

Work Performance

3.1 Agenda (1)	3.2 Work Report (1)	3.3 Work Report Continuation Page (1)
(All Projects)	(All Projects)	(If necessary)
		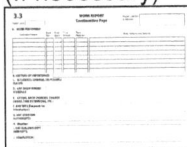

Making Payments

4.1 Conditional Waiver and Release upon Progress Payment (1)	4.2 Unconditional Release upon progress Payment (1)	4.3 Conditional Waiver and Release upon Final Payment (1)	4.4 Unconditional Waiver and Release up Final Payment (1)	4.5 Preliminary Lien Notice Tracking (1)	4.6 Schedule of Values (1)
(All Projects)	(All projects except Maintenance and Repairs)	(All Projects)	(All projects except Maintenance and Repairs)	All projects when Preliminary Lien Notices are received	All projects having several trades under one contract
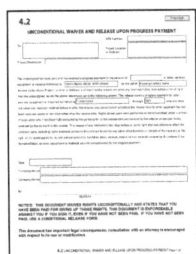		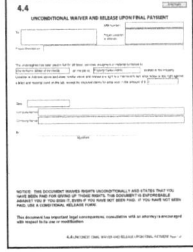			

Tip!
The worksheets in this system have been designed for use with other construction documents or contracts. **For example:** Often construction documents and contract forms are available within specific building jurisdictions and can be obtained from local stationary stores, building department offices or the internet.

Here is a partial list of project participants and/or others who can benefit from using this system:

Property Owner	Architect/Engineer	Real Estate Professional
Property Manager	General or Prime Contractor	Student
Construction Manager	Sub Contractor	Vendor/Supplier
Government (Permits)	Contractor's License Board	Construction Claims (Legal)
Insurance/Bonding Companies	Construction Lenders	Title Companies
Regulatory Agencies	Structural Engineer	Soils Engineer

Here is a list of useful Property and Project information for gathering prior to and upon completing your project:

PROJECT INFORMATION PROJECT DETAILS	PROJECT COSTS	INSURANCE INFORMATION
Project Scope:	Projected Cost:	Company Name
Project Type:	Actual Cost:	Policy Number
Project Classification:		Policy Period
Project Description:	**OTHER INFORMATION**	Effective Date
Desired Start Date:	This is a Rental Property (yes or no)	Expiration Date
Desired Completion Date:	Owner occupied (yes or no)	Personal Liability Amount
Actual Start Date:		Other: similar to project description field
Actual Completion Date:	**PROPERTY PROFILE INFORMATION**	Additional Insured
Substantial Completion Date (For architects):	Information Last Updated:	Additional Insured
Final Lien Release Date:	APN Number: (pre-populates if given)	
One Year Inspection Date:	Owner's Name	
BUILDING PERMIT INFORMATION	Date of last sale:	
Permit Required:	Sale Amount:	
Permit Number:	Property Value:	
Permit Issue Date:	Land Area/SQ FT:	
Permit Expiration Date:	First Loan By:	
Permit City:	First Loan Amount:	
Permit State:	Second Loan By:	
	Second Loan Amount:	

Most of this information can be obtained when using the system in this book and can be extremely useful for overall property transparency and disclosure purposes.

Tip!
For learning how to prepare a schedule for your project refer to the authors' earlier publication "Construction Management Made Easy".

Planning and Resources

Planning and Resources have been combined into one part because one really cannot do one without the other. Planning is necessary to determine resource needs and professional resources are needed to help plan the scope and type of work required for the project. The type and magnitude of the project will determine the order of need for these functions.

PLANNING (1.1)

Planning is usually the first step in the building or improvement process. And depending on the planner the planning process can be approached differently and sometimes become very extensive and involve many steps. But it is the authors' opinion that planning includes answering four basic questions. They are WHO, WHAT, WHEN and HOW.

Who are the resources needed?
What activities and/or components will be needed to begin and complete the project?
When should the project start and be completed?
How much will it cost? And **how** should I pay for it?

The following worksheet has been designed for use as a guide or checklist to help you answer specific questions about your project. Under some circumstances the completed worksheet may be used as a document that describes the scope of work, activities and components needed, thus saving lots of time and costs.

Tip!
Try to develop a clear understanding of your project before it begins.

Models and renderings are sometimes used to understand the project before it begins.

Rendering of Retail Store

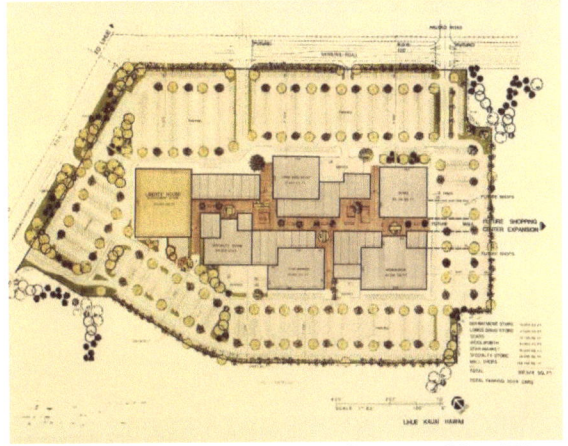
Rendering of Shopping Center Site Plan

1.1 PLANNING

Date: _____ APN Number: _____
To: _____ From: _____ Project Location or Address: _____

Here is a list of activities, components and/or resources needed for this project:

SUPPORT PROFESSIONALS AND SERVICES	YES	NO	MAYBE	COMMENTS
Construction Manager	☐	☐	☐	
Architect	☐	☐	☐	
Interior Designer	☐	☐	☐	
Landscape/Irrigation Architect	☐	☐	☐	
Data/Voice Consultant	☐	☐	☐	
Sound/Acoustical Engineer	☐	☐	☐	
Electrical Engineer	☐	☐	☐	
Mechanical Engineer	☐	☐	☐	
Civil Engineer	☐	☐	☐	
Testing Engineer	☐	☐	☐	
Surveyor	☐	☐	☐	
Traffic Engineer	☐	☐	☐	
Energy Compliance Consultant	☐	☐	☐	
	☐	☐	☐	
	☐	☐	☐	

OFF-SITE IMPROVEMENTS	YES	NO	MAYBE	COMMENTS
Demolition Work	☐	☐	☐	
Curbs and Gutter Work	☐	☐	☐	
Traffic Controls	☐	☐	☐	
Street Widening and Dedications	☐	☐	☐	
	☐	☐	☐	

ON-SITE IMPROVEMENTS	YES	NO	MAYBE	COMMENTS
Demolition Work	☐	☐	☐	
Clearing, grading, fill, and/or dirt removal	☐	☐	☐	
Parking and traffic markings	☐	☐	☐	
Driveways	☐	☐	☐	
Pedestrian Walkways and ramps	☐	☐	☐	
Retaining walls	☐	☐	☐	
Fencing	☐	☐	☐	
Screening for mechanical equipment and trash enclosures	☐	☐	☐	
	☐	☐	☐	
	☐	☐	☐	

Copyright Ponta, Inc. 2010

EXTERIOR UTILITIES AND CONNECTIONS TO BUILDINGS	YES	NO	MAYBE	COMMENTS
Temporary power and utilities to job site during construction	☐	☐	☐	
Power requirement to the building(s)	☐	☐	☐	
Gas service and main meters	☐	☐	☐	
Water service and main meters	☐	☐	☐	
Electric service and main meters	☐	☐	☐	
Storm and sanitary sewers	☐	☐	☐	
Gas service and main meters	☐	☐	☐	
Grease interceptors	☐	☐	☐	
Telephone and data service	☐	☐	☐	
	☐	☐	☐	
	☐	☐	☐	

EXTERIOR IDENTIFICATION AND LIGHTING				
Signs and locations	☐	☐	☐	
Wiring for signs	☐	☐	☐	
Area lighting	☐	☐	☐	
Parking lot lighting	☐	☐	☐	
Bumpers and protection for the above	☐	☐	☐	
	☐	☐	☐	
	☐	☐	☐	

BUILDING SHELL-GENERAL				
On grade	☐	☐	☐	
Raised floor	☐	☐	☐	
Structural framing clear span	☐	☐	☐	
Interior post/columns will interfere with operations	☐	☐	☐	
Special hardware requirements	☐	☐	☐	
Insurance considerations for different roof and wall systems	☐	☐	☐	
Special door and window requirements	☐	☐	☐	
Mezzanine needed	☐	☐	☐	
Delivery docks	☐	☐	☐	
Gutter and downspout requirements	☐	☐	☐	
Delivery docks	☐	☐	☐	
Exterior facade and finish requirements	☐	☐	☐	
Special ventilation requirements	☐	☐	☐	
	☐	☐	☐	
	☐	☐	☐	
	☐	☐	☐	
	☐	☐	☐	
	☐	☐	☐	

Copyright Ponta, Inc. 2010

BUILDING INTERIOR (FLOORING, CEILINGS, PARTITIONS, WALL FINISHES)	YES	NO	MAYBE	COMMENTS
Tile floors	☐	☐	☐	
Carpeted floors	☐	☐	☐	
Hardened concrete with painted surfaces	☐	☐	☐	
Light weight concrete topping	☐	☐	☐	
Terrazzo floors	☐	☐	☐	
Gypsum board ceilings	☐	☐	☐	
Suspended ceilings	☐	☐	☐	
Metal studs for walls	☐	☐	☐	
Wood studs for walls	☐	☐	☐	
Sound attenuation requirements	☐	☐	☐	
Wall protection systems (Corner guards)	☐	☐	☐	
Maintenance considerations when selecting paint	☐	☐	☐	
	☐	☐	☐	
	☐	☐	☐	

MECHANICAL AND ELECTRICAL				
Data wiring	☐	☐	☐	
Voice wiring	☐	☐	☐	
Special electrical wiring	☐	☐	☐	
Special floor or out mounting	☐	☐	☐	
Special meter or transformer locations	☐	☐	☐	
Special electrical requirements	☐	☐	☐	
Special light fixtures	☐	☐	☐	
Foot candle requirements	☐	☐	☐	
Elevator(s) needed	☐	☐	☐	
Power conveyor(s) needed	☐	☐	☐	
Escalator(s) needed	☐	☐	☐	
Insurance considerations for fire sprinklers	☐	☐	☐	
Fire or burglar alarm(s)	☐	☐	☐	
Public address or background music system	☐	☐	☐	
Special fans or pumping system(s)	☐	☐	☐	
	☐	☐	☐	
	☐	☐	☐	
	☐	☐	☐	
	☐	☐	☐	

ENERGY COSTS				
Installed versus life cycle costs for heating and cooling equipment	☐	☐	☐	
	☐	☐	☐	
	☐	☐	☐	
	☐	☐	☐	

Copyright Ponta, Inc. 2010

INTERIOR FINISHING AND FURNISHINGS

	YES	NO	MAYBE	COMMENTS
Special decor for each room	☐	☐	☐	
Special wall treatments, murals, drapes, curtains	☐	☐	☐	
Blending for wall finishes with furniture	☐	☐	☐	
Special furniture, fixtures and equipment placement	☐	☐	☐	
No smoking signs	☐	☐	☐	
Fire extinguishers	☐	☐	☐	
Lockers	☐	☐	☐	
Rest room furnishings and equipment	☐	☐	☐	
	☐	☐	☐	
	☐	☐	☐	
	☐	☐	☐	

LANDSCAPING AND IRIGATION

	YES	NO	MAYBE	COMMENTS
Special types and positions of tress, shrubbery, plants and flowers	☐	☐	☐	
Automatic sprinkler system	☐	☐	☐	
	☐	☐	☐	
	☐	☐	☐	

MATERIALS AND EQUIPMENT-GENERAL

	YES	NO	MAYBE	COMMENTS
Any long lead time items	☐	☐	☐	
	☐	☐	☐	
		☐	☐	
	☐	☐	☐	
	☐	☐	☐	
	☐	☐	☐	
	☐	☐	☐	
	☐	☐	☐	

HOME IMPROVEMENT TIPS FOR SELLING

	YES	NO	MAYBE	COMMENTS
New front door	☐	☐	☐	
Computer match paint touch up or paint interior walls and ceilings	☐	☐	☐	
Rent live plants for interior decoration	☐	☐	☐	
Remove dated wallpaper and paint in neutral color	☐	☐	☐	
Clean and de-clutter (store miscellaneous furniture)	☐	☐	☐	
Update kitchen and baths	☐	☐	☐	
Clean or replace carpeting	☐	☐	☐	
Improve quality of landscaping	☐	☐	☐	
Order and obtain termite inspection report	☐	☐	☐	
Compile all project or improvement information for disclosure	☐	☐	☐	
Obtain City or Local Agencies Selling Requirements:	☐	☐	☐	
Example: Sewer lateral inspection, replacement or repair	☐	☐	☐	
Example: Engergy audit and/or upgrades	☐	☐	☐	
Example: Installation of gas seismic shut off valve	☐	☐	☐	

Copyright Ponta, Inc. 2010

LAND AND BUILDING REQUIREMENTS

Land Size: Acres: _____ Sq Ft _____
Projected Building Size: Sq Ft _____
Land less Building Size equals Remaining Land: Sq Ft _____

AREA PLANNING REQUIREMENTS

RESIDENTIAL		COMMERCIAL/OFFICE/RETAIL/OTHER	
Area Description	SQ FT	Area Description	SQ FT

QUICK COST ANAYSIS

BUILDING VALUATION

SQ FT _____ Times SQ FT COST _____ Equals COST _____
COST _____ Times Cap Rate PER CENT _____ Equals COST/CAP _____
VALUE _____

CONSTRUCTION AND LAND COSTS

LAND SQ FT _____ Times SQ FT COST _____ Equals COST _____
CONSTRUCTION SQ FT _____ Times SQ FT COST _____ Equals COST _____
BUILDING COST _____
VALUE LESS BUILDING COST EQUALS EQUITY IN BUILDING _____

REAL PROPERTY PURCHASE

Profit and Loss Statement	☐	☐	☐	
Real Property Transfer Disclosure Statement	☐	☐	☐	
Appraisal	☐	☐	☐	
Termite Report	☐	☐	☐	
Property Inspection Report	☐	☐	☐	
Zoning	☐	☐	☐	
Grant Deed - Title held	☐	☐	☐	
Tenant Leases (Security Deposits Held)	☐	☐	☐	
Real Property Tax Statements	☐	☐	☐	
Assessments (Streets, Sidewalks, Sewers, etc.)	☐	☐	☐	
Building Set Backs and Easements	☐	☐	☐	
CC&R's (Covenants	☐	☐	☐	
	☐	☐	☐	
	☐	☐	☐	

Copyright Ponta, Inc. 2010

GENERAL REQUIREMENTS FOR CONSTRUCTION PROJECTS

NON-DISTRIBUTABLE LABOR

Item	YES	NO	MAYBE	QTY/UNITS	COST
Project Manager	☐	☐	☐		
Architectural	☐	☐	☐		
Drafting Service	☐	☐	☐		
Interior Design	☐	☐	☐		
Electrical Engineering	☐	☐	☐		
Voice and Data Consulting	☐	☐	☐		
Security System Design	☐	☐	☐		
Sound Engineering	☐	☐	☐		
Mechanical Engineering	☐	☐	☐		
Civil Engineering	☐	☐	☐		
Title 24 Consultant	☐	☐	☐		
Landscape/Irrigation Design	☐	☐	☐		
Soils Engineering	☐	☐	☐		
	☐	☐	☐		
	☐	☐	☐		
	☐	☐	☐		

PERMITS AND FEES

Item	YES	NO	MAYBE	QTY/UNITS	COST
Building Permits	☐	☐	☐		
Gas Fees	☐	☐	☐		
Temporary Power Fees	☐	☐	☐		
Demolition Fees	☐	☐	☐		
Sanitary Sewer Fees	☐	☐	☐		
Domestic Water Fees	☐	☐	☐		
Business License	☐	☐	☐		
	☐	☐	☐		
	☐	☐	☐		

TEMPORARY SERVICES

Item	YES	NO	MAYBE	QTY/UNITS	COST
Overhead Temporary Power Pole	☐	☐	☐		
Temporary Toilet(s)	☐	☐	☐		
Temporary Water	☐	☐	☐		
Temporary Job Phone	☐	☐	☐		
Temporary Job shack and Furnishings	☐	☐	☐		
Temporary Fence and Gate	☐	☐	☐		
Temporary Lighting	☐	☐	☐		
Storage	☐	☐	☐		
Temporary Computer(s)	☐	☐	☐		
	☐	☐	☐		
	☐	☐	☐		
	☐	☐	☐		

Copyright Ponta, Inc. 2010

1.1 PLANNING

OTHER GENERAL REQUIREMENTS	YES	NO	MAYBE	QTY/UNITS	COST
Project Superintendent	☐	☐	☐		
Job Clean Up Labor	☐	☐	☐		
Pick Up Truck for Superintendent	☐	☐	☐		
Debris Removal and Trash Dumpsters	☐	☐	☐		
Time Keeper	☐	☐	☐		
Engineering Layout and Survey	☐	☐	☐		
Construction Staking	☐	☐	☐		
Concrete Testing	☐	☐	☐		
Soils Testing	☐	☐	☐		
Scaffolds	☐	☐	☐		
Small Tools and Equipment Allowance	☐	☐	☐		
Safety Program, Equipment, First Aid	☐	☐	☐		
Project Sign	☐	☐	☐		
Barricades and Cones	☐	☐	☐		
Hauling from Yard	☐	☐	☐		
Watch Person	☐	☐	☐		
Scheduling	☐	☐	☐		
Reconstruction Estimate	☐	☐	☐		
	☐	☐	☐		

INSURANCE AND BONDING

	YES	NO	MAYBE	QTY/UNITS	COST
Workers Compensation Insurance	☐	☐	☐		
General Liability Insurance	☐	☐	☐		
Project Liability Insurance	☐	☐	☐		
Insurance Other	☐	☐	☐		
Performance, Material, and Payment Bond	☐	☐	☐		
	☐	☐	☐		

OTHER OVERHEAD AND CONTINGENCY

	YES	NO	MAYBE	QTY/UNITS	COST
Main Office Overhead	☐	☐	☐		
Project Overhead	☐	☐	☐		
	☐	☐	☐		

PROJECT CLOSE-OUT

	YES	NO	MAYBE	QTY/UNITS	COST
Final Clean Up Labor	☐	☐	☐		
Record Drawings (As-Built Drawings)	☐	☐	☐		
Supervision and Punch List	☐	☐	☐		
Warranties and Guarantees	☐	☐	☐		
	☐	☐	☐		

ONE YEAR INSPECTION

	YES	NO	MAYBE	QTY/UNITS	COST
Supervision and Meeting	☐	☐	☐		
	☐	☐	☐		
	☐	☐	☐		

Copyright Ponta, Inc. 2010

Worksheet 1.1 Explanations

Date This is the date the worksheet was prepared

APN Number
This is the property parcel number assigned by the local authorities

Project Location or Address
This is a description of where the project is located or the actual address including a Job Number if applicable

To/From
Names and addresses of the parties
Support Professionals and Services
As listed
Off Site Development
Any work done outside of your property lines

On Site Development
Any work done inside of your property lines

Exterior Utilities and Connections to the Building
As listed

Exterior Identification and Lighting
As listed

Building Shell-General
The building shell consists of exterior wall and roof systems

Building Interior (Flooring, ceilings, partitions, wall systems)
As listed

Mechanical and Electrical
As listed

Energy Costs
Any activities or items associated with energy conservation or usage

Interior Furnishings and Finishing
As listed

Landscaping and Irrigation
As listed

Materials and Equipment-General
As listed

Home Improvement Tips for Selling
A basic list of fast and easy improvement ideas for getting your property ready to sell

Land and Building Requirements
A basic check list of information to gather when developing a property

Quick Cost Analysis
A fast and easy way of calculating a preliminary value of a property

Real Property Purchase
A basic check list of information to gather when purchasing a property

General Requirements for Construction Projects
A basic check list of possible activities and resources needed for a construction project not usually identified and/or detailed in the contract documents.

HIRING PROFESSIONALS (1.2)

Architects will sometimes qualify contractors on behalf of the property owner while General or Prime Contractors will qualify sub contractors for their own needs. And the property owner usually screens all prime professionals working on their projects. The following worksheet and questions have been designed for the mutual benefit of all parties.

All sections and questions of the worksheet should be completed by the respective professionals and returned. It is generally a good idea to obtain completed worksheets from three to six contractors for a specific project. For minor remodels qualify at least three contractors; and for new home of office buildings qualifying at least six contractors is recommended.

Objectives

As an Owner your objective is to qualify contractors for your specific project. Therefore, you should develop reasonable bidding parameters based on the scope of work or project description for your project. The worksheet has been designed to help define those parameters.

As an Architect, Engineer or Construction Manager your objective is to qualify contractors on behalf of your client;

As a General or Prime Contractor you need to qualify subcontractors; and

As a subcontractor you need to qualify vendors and/or or material suppliers.

Upon qualifying professionals establish your approved contractors list for the purpose of negotiating or bidding your project.

Here are the steps for using these qualification worksheets:

Step One

Select the professionals that you are interested in working with and have them complete their respective section(s) of the worksheet. Give them a reasonable amount of time to complete the worksheet but give them a due date for returning the worksheet.

Upon receiving the completed worksheet review it for completeness and punctuality based on your requested due date. Chances are if the professional can't honor your requested due date to complete a simple worksheet he/she probably can't honor other project commitments either.

Step Two

Contact the references shown on worksheets and ask them the questions.

Step Three

Request written cost proposals from the professionals having the best qualifications and references. And don't be shy about asking the professional to negotiate fees.

Tip!
Use the RFP in this section whenever possible and ask to see a completed project and then look at the details.

A more detailed discussion and scoring method for screening and qualifying Architects and Engineers is covered in the author's earlier publication "Construction Management Made Easy".

Details of a castle built in Japan

1.2 HIRING PROFESSIONALS

Date: _____ To: _____ From: _____ APN Number: _____ Project Location or Address: _____

Here is a checklist for determining whether or not we need construction professionals for this project and if so what type:

PRIME OR MAIN CONTRACTOR

ASK YOUR SELF THE FOLLOWING QUESTIONS:

Question	YES	NO	MAYBE
Do you understand the scope of the work necessary to begin and complete you project?	☐	☐	☐
Are you capable of preparing a written scope of work or specifications for you project?	☐	☐	☐
Do you have the ability to qualify trade professionals and/or subcontractors?	☐	☐	☐
Do you have the time to schedule, coordinate and inspect your project?	☐	☐	☐
Is your project absent of structural alterations or improvements?	☐	☐	☐
Will your project activities allow your specialty contractors to supply all materials, labor and clean-up without your assistance?	☐	☐	☐
Are you able and willing to have the necessary building permit documents prepared, submitted and obtained for your project?	☐	☐	☐
All you willing to assume full responsibility for your project?	☐	☐	☐
Are you capable of setting up, reviewing and approving progress and final payments to contractors?	☐	☐	☐
Do you understand the importance of securing certificates of insurance and lien releases from contractors?	☐	☐	☐
TOTALS:			

If you check NO or MAYBE to five or more of these questions you should consider hiring one of these professionals.

CONTRACTOR OR CONSTRUCTION MANAGER QUALIFICATION INFORMATION

Name: _____ Fed ID/SS#: _____ Bondable (YES or NO): _____
Area of Expertise or Specialization: _____ Bonding Capacity (USD): _____
License Type: _____ Phone Number: _____ Bonding Rate (%): _____
License Number: _____ HTTP:// _____ Work on Hand (USD): _____
License Expiration Date: _____ E-Mail Address: _____

REFERENCES

VENDOR OR CLIENT NAME	PHONE NUMBER	E-MAIL ADDRESS

QUESTIONS TO ASK VENDORS OR CLIENTS

Type of Project(s) Completed: _____ Date: _____ Size (SQ FT): _____ Cost or Budget: _____

Completed the work on Schedule: ☐ YES ☐ NO Comments here Paid Bills on Time: ☐ YES ☐ NO

Copyright Ponta, Inc. 2010

ARCHITECTURAL OR DESIGN SERVICES

ASK YOUR SELF THE FOLLOWING QUESTIONS:

Question	YES	NO	MAYBE
Do you understand the scope of the work necessary to begin and complete you project?	☐	☐	☐
If YES, can you prepare a written scope of work for my project?	☐	☐	☐
If YES, do you have the time and am I willing to prepare the scope of work?	☐	☐	☐
Do you have the expertise to prepare a sketch or drawing(s) for this project?	☐	☐	☐
If YES, do you have the time and am I willing to prepare the sketch or drawing(s)?	☐	☐	☐
Is your project absent of structural alterations or improvements?	☐	☐	☐
Are you willing to assume the liability for planning and designing your project?	☐	☐	☐
Is your contractor capable or willing to prepare scope of work for your project?	☐	☐	☐
Is your contractor capable or willing to prepare the sketch, drawings and specifications for your project?	☐	☐	☐
Will the building permit application require an architect/engineers stamp on the permit documents?	☐	☐	☐
TOTALS:			

If you check NO or MAYBE to five or more of these questions you should consider hiring one of these professionals.

ARCHITECT OR ENGINEER QUALIFICATION INFORMATION

Name: _____ Fed ID/SS#: _____
Experience: _____
License Type: _____ Phone Number: _____ Education: _____
License Number: _____ HTTP:// www. _____
License Expiration Date: _____ E-Mail Address: _____

ARCHITECT/ENGINEER REFERENCES

CM, CONTRACTOR OR CLIENT NAME	PHONE NUMBER	E-MAIL ADDRESS

QUESTIONS TO ASK ARCHITECTS, ENGINEERS, CONTRACTORS OR CLIENTS

Type of Project(s) Completed:	Date:	Size (SQ FT)	Cost or Budget

Notes:

Copyright Ponta, Inc. 2010

Worksheet 1.2 Explanations

Date This is the date the worksheet was prepared

APN Number
This is the property parcel number assigned by the local authorities

Project Location or Address
This is a description of where the project is located or the actual address including a Job Number if applicable

To/From
Names and addresses of the parties

PRIME OR MAIN CONTRACTOR

This section of the worksheet contains a series of questions to ask yourself and depending on the number of YES and NO answers will help you determine whether or not you should consider hiring a prime or main contractor for your project. Remember that all projects are different, so you should probably consider repeating this each time you begin a new project.

CONTRACTOR OR CONSTRUCTION MANAGER QUALIFICATION INFORMATION

This section of the worksheet is used for qualifying all Contractors (Prime or Subcontractors) or Construction Managers. However, questions pertaining to Bonding and License numbers may not apply to Construction Managers because not all construction managers are licensed contractors. Construction Managers as a rule have lots of experience, most likely over 10 years in the construction industry and many colleges and universities offer Construction Management certificate programs and degrees.

CONSTRUCTION MANAGERS

Experience
A minimum of 5 to 10 years of experience is not unreasonable to expect from a Construction Manager.

Education
Many colleges and universities offer certificate programs and degrees in construction management. Copies of certificates of completion and college degrees are desirable.

Work on Hand
This is the total amount of work currently under contract. This amount should represent the total amount of the projects currently being managed by the Construction Manager with a supporting list of corresponding services being performed for each project. The

amount of work on hand should be evaluated with respect to your schedule and the Construction Manager's capabilities and resources.

License Type
This information is optional because Construction Managers generally are not required to be licensed. In California, for example, construction managers are regulated by the contractor licensing laws. However, this varies from state to state and must be verified. But some Construction Managers are licensed Contractors.

License Number
Same as above

License Expiration Date
Same as above

CONSTRUCTION MANAGERS AND CONTRACTORS

Name
Name of Construction Manager or Contractor

Federal or Social Security ID
This information is Optional because many companies or individuals do not welcome giving out this information until they actually have been awarded a contract. It this case, this information should be obtained immediately upon starting the project because it saves time at end of year for tax reporting purposes.

Areas of Expertise of Specialization
Helps define the professionals' qualifications for your specific project

State License Type
For license identification purposes

License Number
To insure that the contractor is properly licensed

License Expiration Date
To insure that the license is currently active and remains valid for the duration of your project

Phone Number
Contact information

HTTP://
This URL is useful for obtaining more information about the company or professional

E-Mail Address
Contact information

Bondable

A contractor is bondable when a rated surety company has given the contractor a written statement of bond ability. Before issuing such a statement the surety company conducts their own background check on the contractor before they make a commitment to provide a bond to the contractor. When the surety company is satisfied that the contractor is a good risk the contractor becomes **bondable**. Even though you may not require a bond for you project you may want to use this information for qualifying contractors. (See Bonding Rate Below)

Bonding Capacity

The bonding capacity is the dollar amount the bonding company is willing to guarantee for all bondable and non-bondable work the contractor has on hand based on the experience level and capabilities of the contractor.

Example: The bonding company determines that the construction company qualifies for a bonding capacity of $2,000,000. The contractor has work on hand, contracts totaling $1,000,000 ($500,000 requiring bonds and $500,000 not requiring bonds). In this example the contractor has a bond surplus of $1,000,000 for any future work requiring a bond and will be granted the bond.

Example: The bonding company determines that the construction company qualifies for a bonding capacity of $2,000,000. The contractor has work on hand, contracts totaling $1,000,000 not requiring bonds. The contractor wants to bid on a new $2,000,000 project requiring a bond, which would increase his work on hand to $3,000,000. In this example the contractor has a bond deficit of $1,000,000 and will not be granted the bond unless the bonding company reevaluates the contractor's capabilities and agrees to increase the contractor's Bonding Capacity.

Tip!

If you are requiring a bond **ask** the contractor to invoice you for its direct cost. **You'll save a hefty mark-up** because it is not necessary to include the bond cost in the contract schedule of values and incur the contractor's markup.

Bonding Rate

When the contractor becomes bondable the amount the surety company charges the contractor for the bond is called the bonding rate. This bonding rate is based on the risk factor the bonding company places on issuing the bond to the contractor. The higher the risks to the bonding company the higher the bonding rate. And conversely, the lower the risks to the bonding company the lower the bonding rate.

The bonding rate is also a good guide for comparing contractors by looking at their bonding rates you can generally tell if the contractor has a good track record.

Example: Contractor A has a bonding rate of 1% (one per cent) whereas contractor B has a bonding rate of 3% (three per cent). Contractor A has a greater experience level and capabilities than contractor B as viewed by the Bonding Company. Also, contractor A's bond will cost you 2% less than contractor B's bond.

Work on Hand
This is the total amount of work currently under contract. A contractor's bonding capacity usually determines an acceptable amount based on a contractor's capabilities.

Job Superintendent Name
This is optional information and is only useful when you have first hand information about a superintendent and you are requesting his/her services on your project.

REFERENCES

When qualifying Prime Contractors or Subcontractors it is good practice to obtain at least three references, preferably from former clients and/or vendors or materials suppliers. And for Construction Manages obtain at least three references from former clients and/or Architects/engineers. These references are needed for obtaining answers to the following questions:

QUESTIONS TO ASK VENDORS OR CLIENTS

Type of Projects completed
Usually you want to hear that the projects completed were similar to your project.

Completion Dates
When were the projects completed? Hopefully the projects were completed within the past couple of years. Earlier is best.

Size of Projects
Usually you want to hear that the completed project(s) were similar in size to your project. Not too big and not too small.

Project Cost or Budget
This is important because it gives you a good idea of the contractor's financial capabilities as it relates to your budget.

Completed the work on schedule
If the work was not completed on schedule how much more time was needed to complete the work and why? It would be nice to hear that the project(s) were completed a head of schedule.

Paid bills on time
This is primarily a question to ask subcontractors, vendors or materials suppliers because generally paying bills on time demonstrates dependability and financial strength.

ARCHITECTURAL, DESIGN OR ENGINEERING SERVICES

It is not uncommon to wonder if you really need an architect, engineer or designer for a particular project. This section of the worksheet contains a series of questions for asking yourself and depending on the number of YES and NO answers will help you determine whether or not you should consider one or all of these professionals. Remember that all projects are different, so you should probably consider repeating this each time you begin a new project.

ARCHITECT OR ENGINEER QUALIFICATION INFORMATION

A/E Name
Name of Architect, Designer or Engineer

Experience
A minimum of 5 to 10 years of experience is not unreasonable to expect from an Architect or Engineer.

Education
Many colleges and universities offer certificate programs and degrees in architecture and engineering. Copies of certificates of completion and college degrees are desirable.

Specialization
Helps define the professionals' qualifications for your specific project

License Type
For license identification purposes because Architects and Engineers are usually required to be licensed, but this varies from state to state and must be verified. In some jurisdictions (depending on the size, number of stories, and structural alterations or additions of a building) architects are permitted to perform the engineering function; and designers are permitted to take on improvement or minor remodel projects.

License Number
If required helps to insure that the Architect/Engineer is properly licensed.

License Expiration Date
To insure that the license is currently active and remains valid for the duration of your project.

Federal or Social Security ID
This information is optional because some companies or individuals are not willing to provide this information until they actually have been awarded a contract. However, it is advisable to obtain this information immediately upon starting the project because it saves time at end of year for tax reporting purposes.

Costing and Contracting

Costing and Contracting have been combined into one part because costs and contract terms and conditions are the major components in preparing a contract. And contracts are work performance expectations in exchange for money or costs.

Expectations

As a property owner your expectations are to have the work completed as scheduled, within the quality standards of the industry, in accordance with the contract documents, and for the costs accepted and agreed upon.

As a General or Prime Contractor, or Subcontractor your expectations, most likely, are to be paid promptly in exchange for completing the work in accordance with the contract document(s).

As a vendor or material/equipment supplier your expectations, most likely, are to be paid promptly when your service and/or merchandise has been delivered and/or installed in accordance with the terms of your Purchase order or agreement.

As a service provider such as an Architect, Engineer, Designer or Construction Manager your expectations, most likely, are to be paid promptly as the work progresses or as determined by your respective agreement.

One of the best ways of accomplishing these expectations is to establish a clear meeting of the minds associated with the project costs and contract or agreement.

The worksheets in this section contain the essentials for achieving these expectations.

The scope, size, and type of project or improvement will determine how and to what extent you use these worksheets. **For example:** If you are doing a home improvement project only a couple of the worksheets would prove useful, whereas if you are constructing or remodeling a building all of the worksheets would prove useful. ("Determining what worksheets to use" in the beginning of this Section I)

RFP (Request for Proposal) (2.1)

There are many methods used for establishing construction costs. Here are three the most common:

1. Using estimating publications based on the type and size of your project;

2. Completing an actual detailed review of the drawings and specifications (sometimes referred to as take-off) listing all the components and activities found; and

3. Requesting and obtaining bids or estimates directly from contractors, vendors and service providers.

Tip!
When obtaining bids or estimates think of them as Cost Proposals because they are only offers until accepted and all proposals must be accepted in writing.

Tip!
When appropriate, reserve the right to reject any and/or all bids for any reason; and to negotiate the contract with any of the bidders.

Usually methods 1 and 2 above are used for budgeting purposes or staying within a given budget during the design and engineering phase and/or to establish a base cost before bidding the project.

This system focuses on using method 3 because methods 1 and 2 are often used on a preliminary basis where as obtaining actual bids or estimates can be finalized, negotiated, and put into a contract or agreement quickly.

The most common way of obtaining these bids or estimates is to request them using a Request for Proposal or RFP (See the Glossary).

Model of a Castle in Japan depicting that there are many components in a structure that need to be identified for costing purposes.

Framing project in California

The following worksheet has been designed to easily gather the pertinent information about your project for requesting costs from your respective professionals:

2.1 RFP (Request for Proposal)

Submit by E-mail | Print Form

Date: _____   APN Number: _____
To: _____   From: _____   Project Location or Address: _____

Your are hereby invited to submit a Cost Proposal for this project.

PROJECT DOCUMENTS AND DELIVERY INSTRUCTIONS

Latest Revision Date: _____   Addenda Number: _____   Proposal Due Date: _____   Time: _____
Obtain Plans and Specifications from: None
Deliver your Proposal to: _____
Phone Number: _____   Phone Number: _____
E-mail: _____   E-mail: _____

DESCRIPTION OF THE WORK

_____

TYPE OF PROPOSAL REQUESTED

☐ LUMP SUM   ☐ TIME AND MATERIALS   ☐ NOT TO EXCEED   Other: _____
Provide Unit Percentage fees for: ☐ Adding (MORE) labor and materials   ☐ Deducting (LESS) labor and materials

REQUESTED ALTERNATE BIDS AND/OR ALLOWANCES

_____

DELIVERY AND/OR COMPLETION OF THE WORK

Starting Date: _____   Starting Time: _____   Other: _____
Completion Date: _____   Time: _____
Deliver Date: _____   Starting Time: _____
☐ Include any lead time items and time needed   ☐ Include the number of calendar days to complete the work

BONDING AND INSURANCE REQUIREMENTS

☐ Bid Bond   ☐ Performance Bond   ☐ Payment Bond   Actual Cost of Bond(S) (DO NOT INCLUDE IN BASE BID): _____
☐ Number of Parties to be named as Additional Insured on Insurance(s) Policies: _____   ☐ See Continuation page for limits

OTHER REQUIREMENTS   ATTACHMENTS

Pre-Proposal site inspection: ☐ YES ☐ NO Other: _____   ☐ **2.2** Procedural Memorandum
Inspection Date: _____   Time: _____   ☐ **2.3** Proposal/ Agreement
Special Instructions: _____   ☐ **2.3a** Terms and Conditions
                                                              ☐ **2.4** Continuation Page
                                                              ☐ _____

Copyright Ponta, Inc 2010   **2.1** RFP (Request for Proposal) Page 1 of 1

Worksheet 2.1 Explanations

Date This is the date the worksheet was prepared

APN Number
This is the property parcel number assigned by the local authorities

Project Location or Address
This is a description of where the project is located or the actual address
Including a Job Number if applicable

To/From
Names and addresses of the parties

PROJECT DOCUMENTS AND DELIVERY INSTRUCTIONS

Latest Revision Date
This is the latest revision date on the Construction Documents.

Addenda Number
If any addendums to the construction documents or RFP have been issued this is the last number issued.

Proposal Due Date/Time
This is the date and time you want to receive your proposal. In some cases proposals are not accepted if one minute late.

Obtain Plans and Specifications From
This is where the contract documents can be picked up by the respective bidders

Deliver your proposal to
This is the location you want your proposals delivered to

DESCRIPTION OF WORK

This is a brief written description of your project. You may choose to leave this blank if construction documents are available. Or you can reference any attachments that describe the scope of work for your project such as sketches, drawings, specifications, etc.

Phone Number/E-mail
Contact information for both parties

TYPE OF PROPOSAL REQUESTED

Lump Sum
See the Glossary

Time and Materials
See the Glossary

Not to Exceed
See the Glossary

Other
Enter any other type of contracting method such as "Not to Exceed" (See Glossary) or "Cost Plus" (See Glossary). There are many ways of structuring contract terms. The important thing is that both parties understand and agree on the structure.

Provide unit percentage fees for: Adding (MORE) labor and materials and deducting (LESS) labor and materials
In the event more or less labor or materials will be needed/not needed to complete your project it is good to know, in advance, how much you will be charged for such changes.

Unit percentage is the percentage rate the contractor will charge in addition to the actual cost of the labor and materials on added or deducted items. **For example:** The unit percentages have been established as 5% for more (additive) work and 2% for less (deductive) work. You have decided to remove (deduct) the carpet from the contract amount. The contractor will prepare a change order request to deduct the cost of the carpet including installation costs plus 2%. And if you were adding the carpet to the contract the contractor would prepare a change order proposal to add the cost of the carpet including installation costs plus 5%.

It is not uncommon for deductive (LESS) unit percentages to be 0% because some contractors feel that they have already spent time and energy on the item and therefore do not want to return any part of their markup on deductive items.

REQUESTED ALTERNATE BIDS AND/OR ALLOWANCES

See Alternate Bid and Allowance in the Glossary. When budgets are tight it is not uncommon to request alternate prices or allowances for components, materials and/or equipment. And sometimes the contractor will submit a bid with his own proposed Alternates or Allowances.

Alternates are useful when you need to compare prices for certain items or if you want to see if specified items can be substituted with an item of equal or better qualities for a lesser price.

Allowances are useful when the component or item specified in unclear. In this case an allowance (cost allowance) for the bid item will be included in the proposal and ultimately the contract. When the actual substantiated cost of the component or item is obtained the following will occur: If the cost is less than the allowance amount the owner would receive a <u>credit</u> for the difference; but if the cost is more than the allowance the contractor would be paid the <u>additional</u> amount.

DELIVERY AND/OR COMPLETION OF THE WORK

Starting Date/Time
This is your desired project starting date and/or time

Completion Date/Time
This is your desired project completion date and/or time

Delivery Date/Starting Time
This is primarily for items being delivered to your project such as materials or equipment.

Other
Enter any reasonable starting or delivery instructions

Include any lead time items and time needed
See <u>Lead Time</u> in the Glossary. It is not uncommon for contractors or vendors to need time to receive items or equipment. Some items need to be fabricated, are back ordered, or have shipping restrictions that take time. Therefore, it is important to know what items require lead time and how much time because this information allows you to make a decision on possibly substituting the item(s) with something else or simply deleting it from the contract documents or scope of work.

Include the number of calendar days to complete the work
Use this section if the schedule is based on the number of days instead of an actual completion date. "Calendar days" are consecutive days whereas "days" alone can be construed as meaning only "Working days.

BONDING AND INSURANCE REQUIREMENTS

Bid Bond
See the Glossary

Contractor's license Bond
See the Glossary

Performance Bond
See the Glossary

Payment Bond
See the Glossary

Actual Cost of Bond
This is the actual cost of the bond without any markup

Number of Parties to be named as additional insured
This is the number of people and/or entities you want named as additional insured's on the certificates or insurance for your project such as the construction lender, contractor, Home owner Association, etc. Usually parties involved in the project ask to be named as additional insured's.

Limits of Insurance
These are the minimum insurance limits that you require for your project. Your insurance underwriter, most likely, would be pleased to provide you with these limits.

Generally, all construction contracts will have a section on insurance stating the property owner's and contractor's insurance obligations under the contract. The worksheets in this system only include contractor's Insurance requirements. But as a rule:

The **PROPERTY OWNER** is generally asked to procure and maintain in full force and effect:

Fire insurance with course of construction, vandalism and malicious mischief clauses usually the sum of at least equal to the contract price with any losses payable to any beneficiary under any deed of trust covering the project. The policies may name the contractor and construction lender as additional insured; and if the owner fails to procure this coverage the contractor generally has the option of procuring the insurance as agent for and at the expense of the owner.

The **CONTRACTOR** is required to have Worker's Compensation and Employer's Liability Insurance as required by the respective contractor licensing states. In California, for example, all contractors are required to procure worker's compensation insurance before a contractor's license is issued. There is one exception to this requirement. If the contractor has no employees, an exemption certificate must be submitted to the Contractors State License Board, certifying under penalty of perjury that he/she does not employ any person in any manner to be subject to Worker's Compensation laws of California.

It is strongly recommended that you contact the Contractor's License Board in your respective state or jurisdiction to confirm these requirements.

All other insurance requirements and limits of insurance are generally determined by the architect and/or the owner and are usually written into the specifications for the project.

Worksheet 2.3 Proposal/Agreement includes a section for minimum Insurance requirements and limits of insurance. And **Worksheet 2.3a Terms and Conditions** include a section for Insurance requirements and limits of insurance.

Tip!
Always demand certificates of insurance from the contractor before he/she starts the work and examine the coverage expiration dates and being satisfied with the amount of coverage the policies offer; **otherwise, you may incur considerable liability.**

OTHER REQUIREMENTS

Pre-Proposal Site Inspection
This is sometimes referred to as a "Pre-Bid Inspection" and as a rule, contractors insist on inspecting a project before submitting a cost proposal or bid because they want to familiarize themselves with the site to be satisfied that there are no existing conditions contrary to the RFP requirements and/or bidding documents. And most property owners would insist on having such an inspection. **An example** of a project not necessarily requiring a site inspection would be an emergency repair such as roof leaks or a faulty water heater repairs.

Inspection Date/Time
The is the date and time you want to hold the site inspection

Special Instructions
Write any special instructions or requirements you deem necessary

ATTACHMENTS

For referencing and including any additional worksheets or information to the page

PROCEDURAL MEMORANDUM (2.2)

When more than one trade contractor or installer is working on the same project they may have different opinions or practices associated with their respective responsibilities under the contract documents. And it is unlikely that the contract documents will address their individual responsibilities or who does what. Also, it is unlikely that the contract documents will address various costing responsibilities. This Procedural Memorandum is designed to clarify <u>before construction begins</u> who does what, when, and who pays for miscellaneous fees such as, but not necessarily limited to, utility connections, clean up, and other performance expectations. Many of the topics covered in this memorandum are usually discussed and established <u>during the construction process</u>. But by having a clear understanding <u>before construction begins</u> saves lots of frustration, negotiation time, and builds project harmony from the beginning.

This Procedural Memorandum includes the following topics:

GENERAL TOPICS	
Purpose	Job Conduct
Working Hours	Safety Meetings and Accidents
Insurance	Protection of the Work during Construction
Payment Requirements	Laws and Codes
Lien Waivers and Releases	Guarantee
Submittals and Substitutions	Verbal Commitments
Project Schedule	
OTHER COSTS	
Bond	Site Inspections
Fees	HVAC (Heating, Ventilation, Air Conditioning)
Meters	Unloading
Items Furnished by others	Stored Materials
Permits	Excavation and related cutting and patching
Pre-Ordered Items	Demolition
Cutting and Patching	Earth Quake Codes
Roof Flanges, Roof Jacks and Pitch Pockets	House Keeping and Clean up
Allowances	Special Instructions

Tip!
Example: A **special instruction** may say "If site cleanliness and dust control is not performed in a timely manner owner shall have the right to have this work done by others at contractor's expense".

Building in Japan completely wrapped during construction

Tip!
Protect you property and the environment by enclosing it while under construction.

2.2 PROCEDURAL MEMORANDUM

Date: _____   To: _____   To: _____   APN Number: _____   Project Location or Address: _____

GENERAL TOPICS

PURPOSE

This **Procedural Memorandum** is intended to clarify any questions about "who does what". They supersede instructions of other bid documents <u>only</u> as they may relate to who furnishes and/or installs specific materials, equipment, fees and services.

This document will become part of the final contract agreement if you are the successful bidder. Submittal of your proposal, without qualifications, implies that you have included all the conditions contained in this document.

WORKING HOURS

Standard Hours of Work Shall be between _____ and _____

Any contractor who needs to work outside of the established hours of work other than stipulated above must have the written approval of PURCHASER's Superintendent and shall be wholly responsible and liable for site security until the next regular hours of work.

All material shipments to the job site must be arranged 48 hours in advance with the Project Superintendent. Contractors are responsible for providing flagmen, if required.

INSURANCE

Prior to the start of work, all required insurance's must be in effect and certificates must be received by PURCHASER. The Certificate of Insurance shall be in forms and of limits as specified in the Contract Documents and/OR contract.

PAYMENT REQUESTS

All payment requests must be received by the [25th] day of the month   Or as follow:

_____

LIEN WAIVERS AND RELEASES

☐ If checked Purchaser will not process payments without receiving Lien Releases
☐ See attached procedure for submitting Lien Waivers and Releases
☐ Lien Waivers and Releases are required for this project
☐ Lien Waivers and Releases are not required for this project
☐ _____
☐ _____
☐ _____
☐ _____
☐ _____
☐ _____

Copyright Ponta, Inc. 2010

SUBMITTALS AND SUBSTITUTIONS

All materials, products, shop drawings, fabrications, manufactured items and equipment will be submitted for the

☐ Architects   ☐ Owners   ☐ Seller   ☐

Submittals should be forwarded to PURCHASER in the following number of copies:

Description	Copies
Text	4
Text	4
Manufacturers Literature	4
Samples	4

TIMELINESS: Prompt forwarding of submittals is required. It is the respective service providers responsibility to provide the required submittals pursuant to the construction schedule allowing for one week review and approval or the submittals. Delays in the construction schedule due to untimely submittals is unacceptable.

SUBSTITUTIONS: It is essential that all substitution requests be submitted **within the first** `3` **days of signing the contract**. Any request for substitution must be marked clearly as a **Request for Substitution**. Any submittal not conforming to the Plans and Specifications or not identified as a substitution will be rejected. Any loss of time or adverse impact on the schedule because of late, incorrect or incomplete submittals will be charged to the contractor.

PROJECT SCHEDULE

The Project Schedule shall be posted or placed in a conspicuous place at the job site or as follows:

JOB CONDUCT

A copy of any contractor's job site Injury and Illness Prevention Program, as required under the respective project State County or City regulations are ☐ Required ☐ Not Required for this project.

The following are prohibited on this Project Job Site:

Radios
Alcoholic Beverages
Glass Bottles
Abusive language or loud profanity

Contractors must comply with the respective project State, County, or City Hazardous Communications Requirements.

Copyright Ponta, Inc. 2010

SAFETY MEETINGS AND ACCIDENTS

All accidents should be reported to the: ☐ Architects   ☐ Owner   ☐ Superintendant

Said accidents should be reported at the time of the accident.

Each contractor should hold at least [1] safety meeting per [Week]

All Contractors using flammable liquids, cutting torches, welders, etc., should furnish their own fire extinguishers for the work.

EMERGENCY fire extinguishers should be placed in the open.

Traffic control, if required, will be the responsibility of:

☐ General Contractor   ☐ Each Subcontractor   ☐ [   ]

PROTECTION OF THE WORK DURING CONSTRUCTION

Each contractor or service provider shall provide protection to existing and new surfaces that may be damaged by their work. Any damages that occur must be restored to new or better than the new condition at the cost of the Contractor.

LAWS AND CODES

All work shall be performed under and in accordance with all applicable governmental codes and requirements, trade practices, and respective facilities rules and/or regulations.

Each contractor or service provider shall pay all taxes or contributions levied by any governmental or other authority on any materials, supplies, labor or equipment, or the use or sale or installation thereof, and the same shall be deemed to be included in the contract price and other costs shall not be entitled to any payment from purchaser on account thereof.

GUARANTEE

Guarantee all materials and workmanship for at least [One] ([1]) year from the :

[Text]

VERBAL COMMITMENTS

PURCHASER will not honor any requests for payment for additional work unless such request is accompanied by a written order signed by an authorized **PURCHASER** representative.

OTHER COSTS

BOND

☐ Do not include the Cost of the Bond(s) in your Base Bid.
☐ Include the Cost of the Bond(s) in your Base Bid.

☐ [   ]
☐ [   ]
☐ [   ]

FEES

Include all tap-in, hookup fees in your bid	☐ Alternate Bid Item When Checked
	☐ Alternate Bid Item When Checked
	☐ Alternate Bid Item When Checked
	☐ Alternate Bid Item When Checked
	☐
	☐

Copyright Ponta, Inc. 2010

2.2 PROCEDURAL MEMORANDUM Page 3 OF 5

METERS

Include all costs for obtaining and installing meters in your bid	☐ Alternate Bid Item When Checked
	☐ Alternate Bid Item When Checked
	☐
	☐
	☐

ITEMS FURNISHED BY OTHERS

Include the cost for accepting delivering, unloading, assembly, storing any items being installed by you but furnished by others.

PERMITS

Include the cost of all permits in your bid	☐ Alternate Bid Item When Checked
	☐ Alternate Bid Item When Checked
	☐
	☐

PRE-ORDERED ITEMS

A pre-ordered item such as materials or equipment have been ordered but have not been paid for. Include the cost of the following items in your bid included shipping and handling.

ITEMS	COST

CUTTING AND PATCHING

Cutting, framing, patching and/or sealing of all required openings in roofs, floors, walls, ceilings and fixtures such as cabinets will be done by the contractor requiring the openings. Or arrangements will be made by that contractor for others to do the work at his sole cost and expense. (**EXCEPTION** Drywall contractors must cut and frame all necessary openings in drywall ceilings.)

ROOF FLANGES, ROOF JACKS AND PITCH POCKETS

Each contractor requiring roof penetrations must include in their bid the costs necessary for any flanges, flashing, framing, pitch pockets and sealing as may be required. (**EXCEPTION** In the case of existing facilities it is **strongly recommended** that the building owner be contacted for the name of his roofing or roofing maintenance contractor).

ALLOWANCES

If allowances are indicated in the specifications or bid documents, include them in your bid and state the amount included

SITE INSPECTIONS

If a site inspection is required by submission of a Bid or Proposal, you acknowledge that you are familiar with the job site conditions affecting the work. Should your investigation of the job site reveal conditions contrary to the plans, specifications or scope of work, you must advise Purchaser in writing prior to or when submitting your bid. Failure to do so will not relieve you from completing the work as shown or required.

HVAC (Heating, Ventilation, Air Conditioning)

HVAC contractor will include the supply and installation of the following:

All condensate lines from units to sewer system
All sheet metal flashing, scuppders, coping, etc.

UNLOADING

Each contractor must include costs for unloading, storing and distributing material furnished for his use, whether furnished by **him self** or **others.**

STORED MATERIALS

Any stored materials shall be identified and/or labeled with the following information:

☐ Project Number	
☐ Project Name	
☐ APN Number	
☐	

EXCAVATION AND RELATED CUTTING AND PATCHING

Contractors will include costs as may be necessary to install any under slab or underground plumbing, mechanical or electrical material and will back fill, tamp and compact excavated areas as necessary. When this work is required under or in existing slabs contractors will include costs for saw cutting (electric saws only if in building interiors), concrete chipping, concrete removal, and concrete patching.

DEMOLITION

Electrical, HVAC, Plumbing and Sprinkler contractors must include all demolition that pertains to their trade. Any architectural demolition, such as walls, ceilings and floor covering, will be performed by **PURCHASER** unless specifically specified otherwise.

EARTH QUAKE CODES

Each contractors or supplier will include costs as may be necessary to install any seismic bracing, compression struts, hangers, and suspension devices deemed necessary by building codes for their respective fixtures, equipment, or systems installation. **For example**, lighting fixture support wires shall be by electrical contractor, suspended ceiling system wiring will be by Ceiling contractor, etc.

HOUSE KEEPING AND CLEAN UP

Each Contractor is responsible for clean up and removal of all debris created by his work. Said clean up and debris removal must be provided on a <u>daily basis.</u> Debris boxes: ☐ Will   ☐ Will Not   be provided.

SPECIAL INSTRUCTIONS

Copyright Ponta, Inc. 2010

PROPOSAL/AGREEMENT (2.3)

This worksheet has been designed to promote standardization and save lots of time reviewing and preparing new agreements. The worksheet can be used as a Proposal, Contract, Purchase Order, or Change Order by simply checking the appropriate box(s). **For example**, if the worksheet is used initially to submit a cost proposal it can be amended immediately by checking the CONTRACT or PURCHASE ORDER box and then executing the agreement.

Or the worksheet can be used to collect and organize information for a project. The worksheet includes all the essentials for collecting costing and scheduling information for your project. This worksheet gathers information for incorporating into the final contract agreement. Or simply check the appropriate box and execute the worksheet.

Even though written communication is <u>stressed</u> and should be the rule of thumb, many contractors (especially subcontractors and material suppliers) will give verbal quotations or proposals on the telephone or sometimes incomplete information is written on the back of a business card. The FAX machine and e-mail have helped enormously to minimize this practice. However, when you do obtain these kinds of quotations or proposals it is extremely important to obtain all pertinent detailed information about the proposed transaction because this information will become the Terms and Conditions written into the final contract agreement and/or purchase order between you and the respective contractor or vendor.

This worksheet has been designed for obtaining the pertinent information necessary for defining and understanding the scope of work, terms and conditions, and any limitations for the project or improvement.

Tip!
If you decided to use another form of agreement such as the Contractor's form of agreement you can easily include your requirements by preparing and attaching a written ADDEMUM. Simply list your requirements, have the contractor review the addendum, and attach it to the contract. Be sure that both parties initial the addendum.

Tip!
When submitting proposals it is good practice to include the expiration date or number of days when the proposal will expire. Use the **QUALIFICATIONS OR EXCLUSIONS** field in this Worksheet for this purpose. Say "This proposal is valid for (X) days from the date of this proposal" or "This proposal will expire on (Date)".

2.3 PROPOSAL/AGREEMENT

Date: [ ]　RFP Dated: [ ]　APN Number: [ ]

☐ PROPOSAL　☐ CHANGE ORDER
☐ CONTRACT　☐ PURCHASE ORDER

Project Location or Address: (Job Number) [ ]

To: [ ]　From: [ ]

Contractor Phone: [ ]　License Number: [ ]　Expiration Date: [ ]
E-mail: [ ]　HTTP:// [ ]
Attended the Pre-Proposal site inspection:　☐ YES　☐ NO　☐ NONE REQUIRED　Other: [ ]

DESCRIPTION OF THE WORK

[ ]

Number of Addendas Received: None　Latest Revision Date: None

PAYMENT

BASE PRICE: [ ]　☐ Tax Included　Per Plans and Specifications:　☐ YES (See Above)　☒ NONE

Cost Type:　☐ LUMP SUM　☐ TIME AND MATERIALS　☐ NOT TO EXCEED　Other: [ ]

☐ Deposit Required　☐ Advance Required　☐ COD Payments Required　☐ FOB Job Site　☐ FOB Installed　☐ FOB Factory

For more or additional work add cost plus (Percent)% 0　　For less or deduct work add cost plus (Percent)% 0

INCLUDED IN THE WORK

☐ Labor and Materials　☐ Labor Only　☐ Materials Only　☐ Supply and Install　☐ Install Only　☐ Supply Only

DELIVERY AND COMPLETION

Starting Date: [ ]　Starting Time: [ ]　Other: [ ]
Completion Date: [ ]　Completion Time: [ ]
Delivery Date: [ ]　Delivery Time: [ ]
Work will be completed within: [ ]　☐ DAYS　☐ WEEKS　From: [ ]
Lead Time Needed: None　☐ DAYS　☐ WEEKS　Because: [ ]

ALTERNATE COSTS

Description	ADD to Base Bid	DEDUCT from Base Bid

QUALIFICATIONS OR EXCLUSIONS

[ ]

AUTHORIZED PARTIES

Contractor Name

Client's Name

Copyright Ponta, Inc. 2010

ATTACHMENTS

☐ **2.2** Procedural Memorandum
☐ **2.3a** Terms and Conditions
☐ **2.4** Continuation Page
☐
☐

2.3 PROPOSAL/AGREEMENT Page 1 of 1

Worksheet 2.3 Explanations

Date
The is the date the worksheet was prepared

RFP Date
Date of RFP if applicable

APN Number
This is the property parcel number assigned by the local authorities

Project Location or Address
This is a description of where the project is located or the actual address including a Job Number if applicable

To/From
Names and addresses of the parties

PROPOSAL
Check this box if you are using the worksheet as a Proposal to complete the work or if this worksheet is simply being used to gather costing information from a contractor or vendor

CONTRACT
Check this box if you want to use the worksheet as the Contract for the project

CHANGE ORDER
Check this box if you want to use the worksheet as a Change Order for the project

PURCHASE ORDER
Check this box if you want to use the worksheet as a Purchase Order for the project

To/From
Names and addresses of the parties

Contractor Phone
Contact information

License Number
To insure that the contractor is properly licensed

License Expiration Date
To insure that the license is currently active and remains valid for the duration of your project

HTTP://
This URL is useful for obtaining more information about the company or professional

E-Mail Address
Contact information

Attended the Pre-Proposal Site Inspection
Check the YES box if the meeting was attended

Other
Enter any other project specific information

DESCRIPTION OF THE WORK

Number of Addenda Received
This is the number of the last Addenda (See Glossary) issued. It is important that all vendors, subcontractors and material suppliers have bid on the same and latest information. Therefore the latest number acknowledges receipt of and inclusion of all addenda's in the proposal.

Latest Revision Date
This is the latest Date that the contract documents have been revised.

PAYMENT

Base Bid
Total contract price

Tax included
For clarifying and/or confirming that tax "is" or "is not" included in the Base Bid

Per Plans and Specifications
Sometimes an item being purchased has not been specified in the project plans or specifications. It is important to know if the item is or is not based on plans and specifications

COST TYPE

There are many types of costing arrangements in Construction Agreements. Here are a couple of the most common included in the worksheet:

Lump Sum
See the Glossary

Time and Materials
See the Glossary

Not to Exceed
See the Glossary

Deposit Required
Deposits usually equal the shipping costs of ordered items and do not include costs for labor and materials. Deposits should be reasonable.

Advance Required
Advance payment amounts for contracts are generally regulated by local or state contracting agencies. You can obtain these allowed advance amounts by contacting your respective local contractor's licensing board.

Tip!
Don't confuse an advance with a deposit. Deposits are generally for ordered items whereas an advance is an amount given to the contractor on the total contract amount. Don't advance more than what is allowed by the local regulatory agencies which is usually a percentage of the contract amount.

COD Payments Required
COD (See the Glossary) When checked this means that COD payments are required.

FOB Job Site
FOB (See the Glossary) When checked this means that the liability for the item(s) changes hands when they arrive and are accepted at the Job site.

FOB Installed
FOB (See the Glossary) When checked this means that the liability for the item(s) changes hands upon completing and accepting the installation of the item.

FOB Factory
FOB (See the Glossary) When checked this means that the liability for the item(s) changes hands upon leaving the respective manufacturing facility.

For more or additional work add cost plus (Percentage)
This is the unit percentage rate the contractor will charge in addition to the actual cost of the labor and materials on added (MORE) items.

For less or deductive work deduct cost plus (Percentage)
This is the unit percentage rate the contractor will charge in addition to the actual cost of the labor and materials on deducted (LESS) items.

INCLUDED IN THE WORK

Labor and Materials
This means that the cost of labor and materials have been included in the total cost.

Labor Only
This means that only the cost for labor has been included in the total cost.

Materials Only
This means that only the cost of the materials have been included in the total cost

Supply and Install
This means that the cost to supply and install the item(s) have been included in the total cost

Install Only
This means that the cost to install a particular item(s) only have been included in the total cost

Supply Only
This means that only the cost to supply the particular item(s) have been included in the total cost

DELIVERY AND COMPLETION

Starting Date/Time
This is the project starting date and/or time

Completion Date/Time
This is project completion date and/or time

Delivery Date/Starting Time
This is the delivery and/or installation starting time for items such as materials or equipment.

Other
These are any other terms and conditions that may apply to the agreement.

Work will be completed within
Use this section if the schedule is based on the number of days instead of an actual completion date above. "Calendar days" are consecutive days whereas "days" alone can be construed as meaning only "working days".

Lead Time Needed
Lead Time (See the Glossary) this is the amount of lead time needed by the contractor or vendor for delivery of an item(s) or to begin the project.

Tip!
Adjust your scheduled completion time based on any lead-time requirements because this makes your schedule realistic and avoids conflicts.

ALTERNATE COSTS

See the Glossary

ALLOWANCES

See the Glossary

QUALIFICATIONS OR EXCLUSIONS

Here is where you note anything to qualify your proposal such as clarifications; or if you are excluding any thing such as, but not necessarily limited to, items, components, activities, work, etc. from your proposal. If you have any doubts or performance concerns list them in this section. **For Example:** If the completion or delivery time of an item compromises the requested completion time as set forth in the bidding documents it may be necessary to qualify the proposal by saying "the completion time is subject to receiving the (item) from the manufacturer by (Date)".

ATTACHEMENTS

For referencing and including any additional worksheets or information to the page

TERMS AND CONDITIONS (2.3a)

These terms and conditions have been designed as an attachment with Worksheet 2.3 PROPOSAL/AGGREEMENT. The PURCHASE ORDER section covers the sale and purchase of merchandise or material and the CONTRACT section constitutes an agreement for the completion of all labor, materials, equipment and services for the project.

Tip!
The use of these Terms and Conditions is optional because other Terms and Conditions may be available from other sources or local regulatory agencies.

RFP and PROPOSAL/AGREEMENT Continuation Page (2.4)

This worksheet is used to continue worksheets 2.1 and/or 2.3. The section on Insurance Requirements makes it easy to include you specific insurance requirements and limits.

2.3a TERMS AND CONDITIONS

Whether this instrument is a PURCHASE ORDER providing only for the sale and purchase of merchandise or material, or does a CONTRACT constitute an agreement for labor and material to be supplied to Purchaser by a Seller is governed by the entries on FORM 2.3. Hereafter set forth are the terms and conditions of governing each transaction.

PURCHASE ORDER

Purchaser reserves the right to countermand or cancel this order, or any part thereof, if delivery is not made on the date specified or if there is a suspension or interruption of the work on the project due to fire, earthquake, casualty, labor dispute or any other case beyond its control.

Material purchased is subject to inspection and will require approval of governing agencies and authorized persons of Purchaser and Purchaser reserves the right to reject the merchandise purchased by reason of damage or defects, in which event it will be held subject to seller's instructions and returned or repaired at seller's expense. No payment will be made for rejected material.

Payment will be made to Seller after delivery and acceptance acknowledged in writing by Purchaser and upon receipt of invoices reflecting proper order number. No charge will be allowed for packing, crating, drayage or storage unless stated herein. This purchase order is non-assignable by seller.

Seller expressly warrants that all the material covered by this order will conform to the description furnished or specified by buyer and will be merchantable, of good material and workmanship and free from defect. Seller expressly warrants that all the material covered by this order, which is the product of the seller, will be fit and sufficient for the purposes intended. If at any time seller has reason to believe that deliveries will not be made as scheduled, written notice setting forth the cause of the anticipated delay will be given immediately to buyer.

Seller guarantees that the material hereby ordered and its sale or use will not infringe any United States or foreign Letters Patent, and seller agrees to defend, protect and save buyer harmless against all suits at law or in equity and from all damages, claims and demands for actual or alleged infringements of any Patent by reason or the sale or use of the material hereby ordered. In the event Buyer must defend any such claim, demand, or suit. Seller agrees to indemnify Buyer for all attorney's fees and costs thereby incurred. In accepting this order seller shall be deemed to represent that the goods to be furnished hereunder were or will be produced in compliance with the requirements of the Fair Labor Standards Act of 1938, as amended. Seller warrants and represents that it is an equal opportunity employer. This purchase order is to be construed according to the laws of the State of the Project location.

CONTRACT

This contract is to be construed according to the laws of the of the State of the Project location. This contract is non-assignable by seller and shall be void in the event of such assignment unless approved in writing by Purchaser. This contract constitutes Seller's offer. It becomes a binding contract on the terms set forth herein, including those on page 1 hereof. No modification of this contract shall be effective unless agreed to in writing signed by an authorized representative of Purchaser.

The contract documents, consisting of but not limited to plans, drawings, specifications or other instruments, are identified on page 1 hereof, Seller agrees that he is familiar with the contract documents, the location of the job site, and the conditions under which the work is to be performed, and he enters into this agreement based upon his investigation of all such matters and is no way relying upon any opinions or representations of Purchaser. This agreement constitutes the entire understanding of the parties. The Contract Documents are incorporated into this agreement by reference.
IN
INDEMNITY Seller agrees to indemnify and save harmless the Purchaser and their agents and employees, and any other party designated by projected specifications, from any and all liability, claims, loss, damages or injuries to any person or to property, including injuries to Seller's employees, and all expenses of investigating and defending against the same: (a) arising from, or connected with the performance of, or failure to perform, the work or other obligations of this contract; (b) caused or claimed to be caused by the independent negligence of the Seller or the concurrent negligence of the Seller with the active or passive negligence of the Purchaser or any other party.

INSURANCE To procure, pay for and maintain at all times during the performance of work under this contract, insurance under forms and through companies and agencies acceptable to Purchaser as follows:

1. Worker's Compensation Insurance as required by law.

2. Comprehensive General Liability Insurance including owned and non-owned auto, contractor's protective, blanket contractual, broad form property damage, and products and completed operations liability coverage, with minimum limits of $1,000,000.00 per occurrence for personal injury claims and $500,000.00 per occurrence for property damage claims, unless higher limits are required by project documengts. The blanket contractual liability insurance coverage shall recognize and insure the indemnity provision above.

3. The Seller shall furnish to Purchaser prior to commencement of work at the project site or within three (3) days after signing this contract, whichever should first occur, Certificates of the insurance required in sub paragraphs 1 and 2 above and which confirm that the policies have been endorsed to provide that Purchaser is named as additional insured for the project under Seller's Comprehensive General Liability policy. All insurance policies shall have a cancellation clause making it mandatory that thirty (30) days written notice be given Contractor before reduction or cancelation in coverage. All required insurance certificates naming Purchaser as additional insured and labor and/or material lien releases shall have been received by Purchaser before any payment is made to Seller.

Seller shall do all work in a first-class and workmanlike manner and to the entire satisfaction of the Purchaser. Seller shall conform in all respects to the provisions of any regulation, ordinance, or local authority that may be applicable to the work, and shall indemnify Purchaser against all penalties by reason of any failure by Seller to so conform.

Seller agrees to promptly begin said work as soon as notified by Purchaser and will conduct the work continuously and with diligence and in strict accordance with Purchaser's directions or with any time schedule it may provide. In case of Seller's failure to successfully perform the work covered by this contract as directed, Purchaser may supply labor and material to carry on the work and deduct the cost of same from any monies due, or which will become due the Seller. ATTENTION IS HEREBY DIRECTED TO THE FACT THAT TIME IS OF THE ESSENCE IN THIS CONTRACT.

Should the Seller fail to employ sufficient competent help to complete the work in the given time, the Purchaser may, after giving forty-eight hours written notice, by letter or e-mail to the last known address of the Seller, employ help to complete the work and charge the same to the Seller's account and/or charge Subcontractor any penalties due to their failure to complete on given due date. If the cost of completing said work exceeds the contract price, the Seller herein agrees to reimburse the Purchaser for any sums over and above the contract price. If the cost of completing the work does not exceed the contract price, any excess shall be paid to the Seller.

Seller agrees to clean-up and remove from project all of his surplus materials and debris remaining after the performance of the work in this contract and as directed by Purchaser; or if not done within three (3) days, Purchaser may remove same and charge actual cost of removal to Seller's account.

All change orders or "extras". If any, or any deviation from the Contract Documents shall be authorized and valid only if approved in writing by Purchaser. Neither party may waive this provision by acts or conduct. Seller guarantees Purchaser against any loss or damage arising from any defect in materials or workmanship furnished under this contract for a period of one year from the date of completion of the project. Seller agrees to comply with all terms and conditions of any construction labor agreement now in existence at the location of the project, and any revision or extension thereof. Unless otherwise provided herein, the stated contract price will be paid in installments as progress payment. Purchaser shall have the right to withhold from the Seller any payments if it fails to present satisfactory evidence that all current bills for labor and materials, or other liabilities, have been paid in connection with this contract. Purchaser shall be entitled to hold Seller's final payment until after final acceptance by Purchaser and until the Seller shall have completed its work to the full satisfaction of Purchaser. No payment made during the progress of the work shall be construed as an approval or acceptance of defective work or improper materials.

In the event legal action is instituted by either party hereto, the prevailing party shall be entitled to reasonable attorney's fees and costs. The Purchaser and Seller for themselves, their agents, personal representatives, and authorized assigns hereby agree to the full performance of the covenants and agreements of this contract

2.4 RFP and PROPOSAL/AGREEMENT Continuation Page

Date: ☐

☐ For **2.1** RFP (Request for Proposal)
☐ For **2.3** PROPOSAL/AGREEMENT
☐

APN Number:
Project Location or Address:

This page when used as an attachment shall, by this reference, be made a part thereof.

DESCRIPTION OF THE WORK

ALTERNATE COSTS

Description	ADD to Base Bid	(DEDUCT) for Base Bid

ALLOWANCES

Description	Allowance Amount

QUALIFICATIONS OR EXCLUSIONS

INSURANCE REQUIREMENTS

General Liability

General Agregatge Limit	$1,000,000.00
Products Completed Operations	$1,000,000.00
Personal and Advertising Injury	$1,000,000.00
Each Occurance Limit	$1,000,000.00
Fire Damage Limit	$50,000.00
Medical Expenses Limit	$50,000.00

Automobiles

Any Auto	$1,000,000.00
All Owned Autos	$1,000,000.00
Scheduled Autos	$1,000,000.00
Hired Autos	$1,000,000.00
	$1,000,000.00
	$1,000,000.00

Other

Hired Autos

Non-Owned Autos	$1,000,000.00
Garage Liability	$1,000,000.00
	$1,000,000.00

Copyright Ponta, Inc. 2010

2.4 CONTINUATION PAGE Page 1 of

Worksheet 2.4 Explanations

Date
This is the same date as the worksheet it is being continued from

APN Number
Same as the worksheet it is being continued from

For 2.1 RFP
Check this box if the this worksheet is being continued from WORKSHEET 2.1

For 2.3 Proposal/Agreement
Check this box if the this worksheet is being continued from Worksheet 2.3 Proposal/Agreement

DESCRIPTION OF THE WORK

Continue the work description from the worksheet being continued from

ALTERNATE COSTS

Continued from the worksheet being continued from

ALLOWANCES

Continued from the worksheet being continued from

QUALIFICATIONS OR EXCLUSIONS

Continued from the worksheet being continued from

INSURANCE REQUIREMENTS

This section includes an editable list of insurance limits. Your insurance agent can provide you with the desirable limits for your specific project.

COMPARING BIDS (2.5)

This worksheet has been designed for the purpose of comparing bids or cost proposals easily. The information is easily collectable from Worksheet 2.3 Proposal/Agreement.

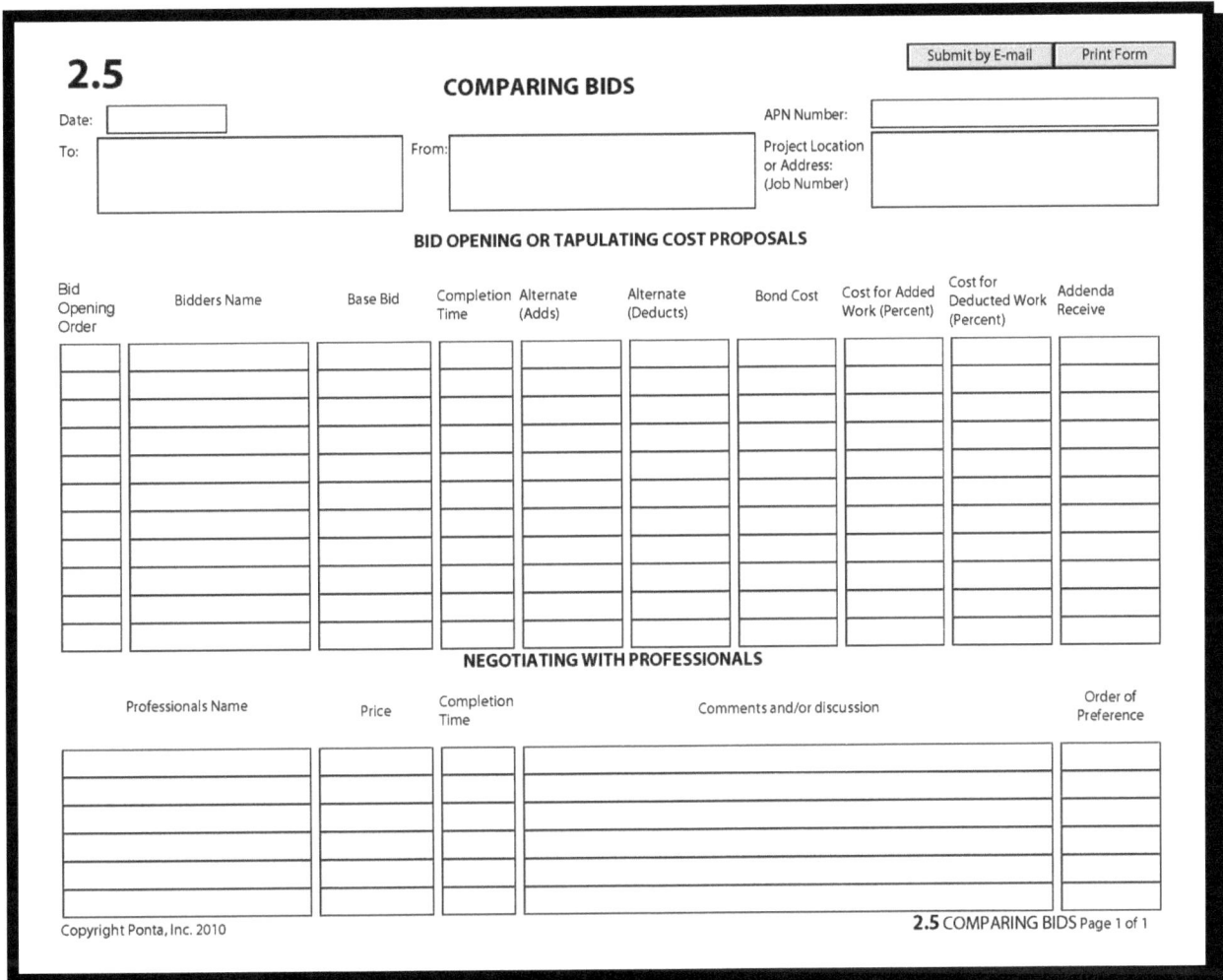

Worksheet 2.5 Explanations

Date
This is the date of the worksheet and date you opened the bids

APN Number
This is the property parcel number assigned by the local authorities

To/From
Name and address of receiving party

Project Location or Address
This is a description of where the project is located or the actual address

BID OPENING OR TABULATING COST PROPOSALS

Bid Opening Order
This is the order in which the bids were opened. This is simply a formality but is good practice because sometimes bidders may be present for a bid opening and this demonstrates fairness.

Bidders Name
This is the name of the person or company submitting the bid or proposal

Base Bid
This is the total price for the work subject to any changes in accordance with the bidding documents such as additive or deductive costs, change orders during construction, any accepted alternates, etc.

Completion Time
This is the amount of time the contractor wants to complete the work

Alternate (Adds)
This is the total cost amount for all Alternates, if and when accepted, that will be added to the Base Bid. It is also desirable to itemize these alternates for each Bidder.

Alternate (Deducts)
This is the total cost amount for all Alternates, if and when accepted, that will be deducted from the Base Bid. It is also desirable to itemize these alternates for each Bidder.

Bond Cost
This is the actual cost of the Performance and/or Payment Bond for this project. Remember, the higher the risks to the bonding company the higher the bonding rate. And conversely, the lower the risks to the bonding company the lower the bonding rate.

Tip!
The cost of the bond is a direct reflection of the bonding rate which means contractors with higher bonding rates and costs are riskier than those with lower bonding rates and costs. But don't use this as the sole determining factor when qualifying contractors.

Cost for Added Work (Percentage)
This is the percentage rate markup the contractor will add to the labor and/or materials costs for approved additional work change orders.

Cost for Deductive Work (Percentage)
This is the percentage rate markup the contractor will add to the labor and/or materials costs for approved deductive work change orders. Remember, it is not uncommon for contractors to <u>return only the actual costs</u> of the labor and materials included in their bid and enter zero (0) here.

Addenda Received
This is the latest addenda number received by the contractor. It is important that the contractor has received any and all addenda issued during the bidding period. If no Addendums were issued enter None or N/A.

NEGOTIATING WITH PROFESSIONALS

Professional Name
This is the name of the construction professional you are negotiating with. It may be one of the Bidders above.

Price
This is the negotiated price to complete your project.

Comments and/or discussion
List any discussion or key comments as part of your negotiations.

Preference Order
Indicate what professional you feel most comfortable with, and the decision may not necessarily be based on the price.

The following is a sample of a completed BID OPENING OR TABULATING COST PROPOSALS section of the worksheet:

Bid Opening Order	Bidders Name	Base Bid	Completion Time	Alternate (Adds)	Alternate (Deducts)	Bond Cost	Cost for Added Work	Cost for Deducted Work	Addenda Receive
1	Smith	$250,000	6 months	$10,000	$1,500	1.0 %	10%	5%	Yes
2	Jones	$225,000	5 months	$9,000	$2,000	1.5 %	8%	5%	Yes
3	Barker	$250,000	6.5 months	$8,000	$1,000	2.0 %	10%	8%	Yes
4	Wilson	$200,000	5 months		$1,000	.75 %	11%	10%	No
5	Hancock	$235,000	4 months	$4,000	$2,000	.50%	6%	0%	Yes

Tip!
To easily calculate the estimated fair market value(s) of your project discard the high and low Base Bids and calculate the average of the remaining Base Bids.

Work Performance

All parts of this system are important but without work performance you basically have little project success. And with good work performance you will, most likely, have a very successful project.

Even though the work is based on the construction documents the parties, owner and contractor, may or may not have the same communication skills and work performance objectives. Therefore, this part of the system includes two worksheets covering <u>before</u>

construction begins (Pre-construction); <u>after</u> construction begins (Course of Construction); <u>when</u> construction is ending (Project Closeout); and <u>one year following the date of completion</u> (one year inspection).

It is the authors' opinion that good communication and reporting systems promote good work performance because questions are being answered in a timely manner and the respective parties are held accountable for their respective responsibilities under the contract documents. Hence the following worksheets have been designed to achieve this degree of communication:

AGENDA (3.1)

This worksheet has been designed for conducting construction meetings. Generally there are four types of meetings. They are "pre-construction" when all parties meet before construction begins; "course of construction" when all parties meet on a scheduled frequency after construction begins until project completion; "project closeout" when all parties meet to request and/or obtain all of the required closeout documents such as, but not necessarily limited to, warrantees, guarantees, equipment manuals, record drawings, and more; and a "one year inspection" when all parties meet for the purpose of conducting an inspection of the project one year following the actual date of completion.

This worksheet provides a basic checklist of topics for these four meeting types.

Tip!
Prepare a sushi bento lunch for your meetings because they are very healthy and easy to share with others. (See the Sushi Section)

Made in Japan

Made in USA

3.1 AGENDA

Submit by E-mail | Print Form

Meeting Date: ____
Start Time: ____ End Time: ____
☐ Pre-Construction Meeting
☐ Course of Construction Meeting
☐ Project Closeout Meeting
☐ One Year Inspection

APN Number: ____
Project Location or Address: ____

Other ____

TOPICS FOR DISCUSSION

☐ Working hours established
☐ Safety Program established
☐ Building Permit Issued
☐ Schedule complete and posted
☐

☐ Notice to proceed with the work issued
☐ Contractor Business Licence
☐ FORM 3.2 Work Report
☐
☐

Other: ____

EMERGENCY CONTACT INFORMATION

Classification	Name and/or Company	Telephone	E-mail
Electrical			
Mechanical			
Plumbing			
Fire Protection			
Project Manager			
Superintendent			
Utility Company			

PROJECT CLOSEOUT

☐ Punch list completed or pending
☐ Warranties and Guarantees
☐ Record Drawings
☐ Final Clean Up
☐ Confirm one year inspection date
☐ Substantial or Final Completion Date

☐ Certificate of Occupancy
☐
☐
☐
☐
☐

Other: ____

Copyright Ponta, Inc. 2010

Worksheet 3.1 Explanations

Meeting Date
This is the actual meeting date

Start Time
This is the time the meeting began

Finish Time
This is the time the meeting ended

APN Number
This is the property parcel number assigned by the local authorities

Pre-construction Meeting
Check this box if the meeting is being held before the scheduled construction start date

Tip!
If not already covered in the contact make it clear that any costs associated with any re-inspections by building officials or hired professionals will be the contractor's responsibility.

Course of Construction Meeting
Check this box if the meeting is being held after the actual start of construction date

Project Closeout Meeting
This meeting is held for the purpose of requesting and/or obtaining all of the required closeout documents such as warrantees, guarantees, equipment manuals, record drawings, final building department sign-off cards, certificate of occupancy, and more. This meeting is generally held prior to the owner taking occupancy meaning prior to the Date of Completion or Substantial Completion (See the Glossary).

One year Inspection Meeting
Check this box if the meeting is being held for the purpose of conducting a one year inspection. This meeting is held one year following the actual date of completion. Usually the items or issues include, but are not necessarily limited to, electrical issues or lights not working, stress cracks above doors and windows, failing materials and/or equipment, paint peeling, door latches not working properly, plumbing and/or condensation leaks.

Tip!
During this inspection note any discovered or observed construction deficiencies and handle them as separate issues.

Other
Describe any other type of meeting.

Project Location and Address
This is a description of where the project is located or the actual address

TOPICS FOR DISCUSSION

The most common topics have been listed.

EMERGENCY CONTACT INFORMATION

Tip! For Owners
Have the contractor provide a sub-contractor's list of emergency telephone numbers because this saves time and frustration when instant communication is necessary.

PROJECT CLOSEOUT

Too often Project Closeout is overlooked. Therefore, this worksheet includes a section devoted entirely to Project Closeout and the most common topics associated with it.

Tip!
Persist in a certificate of occupancy by the governing authority prior to contractor receiving final payment because you'll be assured that work has been completed to code.

Tip!
Ask for written confirmation from the contractor stating "all inspection list (punch list) items have been completed". Otherwise, items may be missed and a re-inspection may be necessary.

WORK REPORT (3.2)

This worksheet has been designed for use by any party performing a review or inspection of the project site. The primary purpose of this worksheet is to record the observed job site conditions. Ideally this worksheet is completed on a daily basis. And as a rule the worksheet should be completed with both owner and contractor representatives present. (See Daily Construction Report in the Glossary)

WORK REPORT Continuation Page (3.3)
This worksheet is used to continue worksheet 3.2.

Worksheet 3.2 Explanations

Report Date
This is the date of the report and date of the reported observations

APN Number
This is the property parcel number assigned by the local authorities

To/From
Names and Addresses of the parties

Project Location or Address
This is a description of where the project is located or the actual address

A. WORK PERFORMED

Contractor/Vendor
Company name for tracking purposes

Total Men
Number of workers observed

Total Hours
Number of hours the above worked

Time Arrived
Workers arrival time

Time work started
This is the actual time the work began

Time Departed
The is the time the workers departed the job site

Time work ended
This is the actual time the work ended

Work Performance/Remarks
Write any worthy positive or negative observations or anything unusual or questionable

B. VISITORS OF IMPORTANCE

Names of any visitors to the job (inspectors, architect, engineers, building officials, owner's representatives, anyone observed)

C. ACCIDENTS, DAMAGE OR ANY POSSIBLE CLAIMS

Important for possible future claims

D. ANY WORK BEHIND SCHEDULE

Important for schedule tracking

E. EXTRAS, BACK CHARGES, CHANGE ORDERS, TIME EXTENSIONS

Important for anticipating potential additional costs or time necessary to complete the project

ANY RFI'S (REQUESTS FOR INFORMATION)

Useful for keeping open communication and clarifying potential issues

G. ANY OVERTIME AUTORIZED

Record to substantiate overtime work

H. WEATHER

Indicate weather conditions at the time of completing the worksheet

I. ANY BUILDING DEPARTMENT SIGN OFFS

For recordation purposes because building permit cards tend to get misplaced or damaged during construction. Indicate what was signed off and the date it was signed.

J. COMPLETION

Substantial Completion Date
(See the Glossary) A date usually determined by the architect

Final Inspection Date
(See the Glossary)

Actual Completion Date
(See the Glossary)

Report Prepared By
This is the name of the person preparing the worksheet

Making Payments

This part of this system is based on paying for performance which is covered in more detail in the authors' earlier publication "Construction Management Made Easy". As work progresses on the project and is completed the contractor expects and is entitled to receive <u>progress payments</u> or other <u>stipulated payments</u> in accordance with the contract documents and/or agreement. And when said payments are made the owner expects to receive a lien free project.

Tip! For Owners
Require an <u>itemized</u> Schedule of Values (See the Glossary) to include, but not necessarily limited to General Conditions, trade activities, bonds at cost, and overhead and profit because this is an invaluable aid in reviewing payment requests. (See 4.6 SAMPLE SCHEDULE OF VALUES at the end of this section).

PAYMENTS AND LIENS

Too often property owners are not aware that if bills are not paid in full for labor, materials, equipment and services or to be furnished for a project, a mechanics lien can be placed against their property even if they paid the prime or main contractor in full.

You may want to check with your local agencies to learn what the mechanics lien consequences are in your specific area. In general a mechanics lien when enforced through a court foreclosure proceeding can lead to the loss of all or part of a property.

Basically there are two types of lien releases. They are: "Conditional" meaning that the payment request is being released subject to the contractor receiving payment; and "unconditional" meaning that the payment request is being released without any conditions. For example: The first payment request would most likely be covered by using a Conditional release because no money has changed hands. A check would have been written and issued for the payment in exchange for the release but not cashed. After the check has been cashed it would be safe for the contractor to provide an unconditional release for that payment.

As a rule lien releases are required in the contract documents or agreements. But a procedure for obtaining them is usually not provided.

Architects, Contractors and Construction managers generally know the procedure but many property owners do not.

The following procedure includes Conditional and Unconditional lien waiver and releases covering <u>progress</u> and <u>final</u> payments:

PROGRESS PAYMENTS

Commencing with the first progress payment request, CONTRACTOR shall submit a CONDITIONAL WAIVER AND RELEASE UPON PARTIAL PAYMENT **(Work Sheet 4.1)** covering all approved scheduled payments to respective subcontractors, material suppliers, and the contractor's general conditions;

Commencing with the second progress payment request and all subsequent progress payment requests, CONTRACTOR, SUBCONTRACTORS and MATERIAL SUPPLIERS shall submit, via the CONTRACTOR, appropriate affidavits and waivers and releases as follows:

Subcontractors and material suppliers shall submit UNCONDITIONAL WAIVERS AND RELEASES **(Worksheet 4.2)** evidencing payment by the CONTRACTOR for all labor and materials covering the previous payment request; and

CONTRACTOR shall submit a CONDITIONAL WAIVER AND RELEASE UPON PARTIAL PAYMENT **(Worksheet 4.1)** covering all approved scheduled payments to respective subcontractors, material suppliers, and all contractors' general conditions.

FINAL PAYMENT

Contractor, Subcontractor and Material Suppliers shall submit, via the CONTRACTOR, appropriate affidavits and wavers and releases as follows:

Subcontractors and Material Suppliers shall submit UNCONDITIONAL WAIVERS AND RELEASES UPON FINAL PAYMENT **(Worksheet 4.4)** evidencing payment by the CONTRACTOR for all labor and materials covering and associated with OWNER'S project; and CONTRACTOR shall submit a CONDITIONAL WAIVER AND RELEASE UPON FINAL PAYMENT **(Worksheet 4.3)** covering all approved contract costs.

<u>The foregoing procedure on Making Payments including the referenced and following WAIVER AND RELEASE worksheets have important legal consequences; consultation with an attorney is strongly encouraged with respect to their use or modification.</u>

Tip!
Request a <u>Conditional Waiver and Release upon Partial Payment Requests</u> from the prime contractor and sub-contractors filing Preliminary Lien Notices (See the Glossary) because your lien exposure will be reduced substantially.

Tip!
For smaller projects, like home improvement projects, and/or purchasing supplies and/or equipment make a check payable to all parties associated with the purchase such as the "Constrictors' Name" and "Suppliers Name". And be sure to use the word "and". This will insure that all parties have been paid and your cancelled check will serve as proof of payment.

4.1

CONDITIONAL WAIVER AND RELEASE UPON PROGRESS PAYMENT

APN Number: [ ]

To: [ ]

Project Location or Address: [ ]

Project Description [ ]

Upon receipt by the undersigned of a check from [Purchasers Name] in the amount of $ [ ] payable to [Payees Name] and when the check has been properly endorsed and has been paid by the bank upon which it is drawn, this document shall become effective to release any mechanic's lien, stop notice or bond right the undersigned has on the job of [Property Owners Name] located at the above Project Location or Address to the following extent. This release covers a progress payment for labor, services, equipment or materials furnished to [Clients Name] through [Date] only and does not cover any retentions retained before or after the release date; extras furnished before the release date for which payment has not been received; extras or items furnished after the release date. Rights based upon work performed or items furnished under a written change order which has been fully executed by the parties prior to the release date are covered by this release unless specifically reserved by the claimant in this release. This release of any mechanic's lien, stop notice, or bond right shall not otherwise affect the contract rights, including the rights between parties to the contract based on a rescission, abandonment, or breach of the contract, or the right of the undersigned to recover compensation for furnished labor, services, equipment, or material covered by this release if that furnished labor, services, equipment, or materials was not compensated by the progress payment. Before any recipient of this document relies on it, said party should verify evidence of payment to the undersigned.

Date [ ]

Company Name: [ ]

Name and Title: [ ]

By: _____
Signature

This document has important legal consequences; consultation with an attorney is encouraged with respect to its use or modification.

4.1 CONDITIONAL WAIVER AND RELEASE UPON PROGRESS PAYMENT

4.2

UNCONDITIONAL WAIVER AND RELEASE UPON PROGRESS PAYMENT

APN Number: _____

To: _____

Project Location or Address: _____

Project Description _____

The undersigned has been paid and has received a progress payment in the amount of _____ or labor, services, equipment or material furnished to [Clients Name (Maker of the check)] on the job of [Property Owners Name] located at the above Project Location or Address and does hereby release pro tanto any mechanic's lien, stop notice or bond right that the undersigned has on the above referenced job to the following extent. This release covers a progress payment for labor, services, equipment or materials furnished to [Clients Name] through [Date] only and does not cover any retention retained before or after the release date; extras furnished before the release date for which payment has not been received; extras or items furnished after the release date. Rights based upon work performed or items furnished under a written change order which has been fully executed by the parties prior to the release date are covered by this release unless specifically reserved by the claimant in this release. This release of any mechanic's lien, stop notice, or bond right shall not otherwise affect the contract rights, including rights between parties to the contract based on rescission, abandonment, or breach of the contract, or the right of the undersigned to recover compensation for furnished labor, services, equipment or material covered by this release if that furnished labor, services, equipment or material was not compensated by the progress payment.

Date _____

Company Name: _____

Company Name: _____

By: _____
Signature

NOTICE: THIS DOCUMENT WAIVES RIGHTS UNCONDITIONALLY AND STATES THAT YOU HAVE BEEN PAID FOR GIVING UP THOSE RIGHTS. THIS DOCUMENT IS ENFORCEABLE AGAINST YOU IF YOU SIGN IT, EVEN IF YOU HAVE NOT BEEN PAID. IF YOU HAVE NOT BEEN PAID, USE A CONDITIONAL RELEASE FORM.

This document has important legal consequences; consultation with an attorney is encouraged with respect to its use or modification.

4.3

CONDITIONAL WAIVER AND RELEASE UPON FINAL PAYMENT

To: _____

APN Number: _____

Project Location or Address: _____

Project Description: _____

Upon receipt by the undersigned of a check from [Clients Name (Maker of the check)] in the sum of _____ payable to [Payees Name] and when the check has been properly endorsed and has been paid by the bank upon which it is drawn, this document shall become effective to release pro tanto any mechanic's lien, stop notice or bond right the undersigned has on the job of [Property Owners Name] located at the above Property Location or Address. This release covers the final payment to the undersigned for labor, services, equipment or material furnished on the job, except for disputed claims for additional work in the amount of $ [0]. Before any recipient of this document relies on it, the party should verify evidence of payment to the undersigned.

Date: _____

Company Name: _____

Company Name: _____

By: _____
Signature

This document has important legal consequences; consultation with an attorney is encouraged with respect to its use or modification.

4.3 CONDITIONAL WAIVER AND RELEASE UPON FINAL PAYMENT

4.4

UNCONDITIONAL WAIVER AND RELEASE UPON FINAL PAYMENT

[Print Form]

To: [   ]

APN Number: [   ]

Project Location or Address: [   ]

Project Description: [   ]

The undersigned has been paid in full for all labor, services, equipment or material furnished to [Clients Name (Maker of the check)] on the job of [Property Owners Name] located at the Property Location or Address above and does hereby waive and release any right to a mechanic's lien, stop notice or any right against a labor and material bond on the job, except for disputed claims for extra work in the amount of $ [0]

Date: [   ]

Company Name: [   ]

Company Name: [   ]

By: _____
Signature

NOTICE: THIS DOCUMENT WAIVES RIGHTS UNCONDITIONALLY AND STATES THAT YOU HAVE BEEN PAID FOR GIVING UP THOSE RIGHTS. THIS DOCUMENT IS ENFORCEABLE AGAINST YOU IF YOU SIGN IT, EVEN IF YOU HAVE NOT BEEN PAID. IF YOU HAVE NOT BEEN PAID, USE A CONDITIONAL RELEASE FORM.

This document has important legal consequences; consultation with an attorney is encouraged with respect to its use or modification.

4.4 UNCONDITIONAL WAIVER AND RELEASE UPON FINAL PAYMENT

TRACKING PRELIMIARY LIEN NOTICES (4.5)

The following sample has been prepared as guide for developing your own calculating spread sheet for the purpose of keeping track of the Preliminary Lien Notices (See the Glossary) received for your project.

PRELIMINARY LIEN NOTICE TRACKING

Company Names	Preliminary Lien Notice Amount	Final Payment (Yes or No)	PAYMENT APPLICATION NUMBER AND AMOUNT								Payments Made	Balance to Pay
			1	2	3	4	5	6	7	8		
ABC Plastering	$50,000		$5,000								$5,000	$45,000
XYZ Concrete	$20,800		$4,000	$1,000							$5,000	$15,800
Fast Plumbing	$10,000	Yes	$5,000	$2,000	$3,000						$10,000	$0
XYZ Mechanical	$30,000										$0	$30,000
Best Drywall	$30,000										$0	$30,000
Totals	$140,800		$14,000	$3,000	$3,000	$0	$0	$0	$0	$0	$20,000	$120,800

SCHEDULE OF VALUES (4.6)

The following sample has been prepared as a guide for developing your own calculating spread sheet for the purpose of keeping track of the Contract values for your project.

SCHEDULE OF VALUES

Activity or Description of Work	Scheduled Value	Inspection Date	Percent Complete	Total Completed Value	Previous Payments	Amount To Pay	Less Retainage 10%
General Conditions	$20,000	6/5/2011	55%	$11,000	$10,000	$1,000	900
Foundations	$100,000	6/5/2011	100%	$100,000	$70,000	$30,000	27,000
Framing	$200,000	6/5/2011	50%	$100,000	$65,000	$35,000	31,500
Drywall	$60,000	6/5/2011	25%	$15,000	$20,000	$(5,000)	$(4,500)
Electrical	$250,000	6/5/2011	50%	$125,000	$6,000	$119,000	$107,100
Plumbing	$240,000	6/5/2011	25%	$60,000	$10,000	$50,000	$45,000
HVAC	$100,000	6/5/2011	60%	$60,000	$15,000	$45,000	$40,500

Activity or Description of the Work
This is the construction cost item or component being observed for payment

Scheduled Value
This is the initial cost value for the above as provided by the contractor. This value does not change. If there is a change order associated with this item or component it is recommended that a new line item be created when the change order has been approved.

Inspection Date
This is the date the item or component was inspected.

Per Cent Complete
This is the observed per cent of completion for the item or component at the time of the inspection.

Total Completed Value
This is the calculated completed value of the Scheduled Value and the Per Cent Complete

Previous Payments
This is the total of any payments previously made to the contractor for this particular item or component

Amount to Pay
This is the calculated amount you should pay before any agreed upon retention for this particular item or component. It is calculated by subtracting the Previous Payment from the Total Completed Value.

Less Retainage
This is the actual calculated amount you should pay for this particular item or component for this payment request if you are holding retention for this project. It is calculated by subtracting the agreed upon retention (10% shown in this example) from the Amount to Pay.

Tip!
Your project is like a castle and is a huge investment, so protect it with proper payment procedures.

Castle in Japan

Glossary

Activity (1) A scheduling term (2) The smallest work unit within a project; the basic building block of a project. (See Project)

Actual Completion Date (1) A loose term used to distinguish between the Date of Substantial Completion (See Date of Substantial Completion) (2) Some projects do not employ architects and thus will not have a Substantial Completion Date. But such projects would have an Actual Completion Date when all of the terms and conditions of the agreement, the work, and Punch List Items (See Inspection List) have been completed and accepted by the owner.

ADA The Americans with Disabilities Act which gives civil rights protection to individuals with disabilities similar to those provided to individuals on the basis of race, color, sex, national origin, age, and religion. It guarantees equal opportunity for individuals with disabilities in public accommodations, employment, transportation, State and local government services, and telecommunications.

Addendum (Addenda) Written information adding to, clarifying or modifying the bidding documents. An addendum is generally issued by the owner to the contractor during the bidding process and as such, addenda are intended to become part of the contract documents when the construction contract is executed.

Agent One authorized by a client (principal) to act in his/her stead or behalf and owes the client a "fiduciary duty" (Trust). Example: Construction Manager for fee but classified as an independent contractor for tax purposes. A construction manager for fee does not have any financial responsibility whereas a construction manager at-risk does have financial risk similar to a general contractor.

Agreement An arrangement between the parties regarding a method of action.

Allowance A term used during the bidding process that means establishing a value for a particular construction component or item and then usually incorporated into the agreement. When the actual substantiated cost of the component or item is obtained the following will occur: If the cost is less than the allowance amount the owner would receive a credit for the difference; but if the cost is more than the allowance the contractor would be paid the additional amount.

Alterations (1) A term used to describe partial construction work performed within an existing structure (2) Remodeling without a building addition.

Alternate Costs (sometimes referred to as Alternate Bid) A term used during the bidding process to identify possible substitute components or items and their associated costs from those specified in the RFP or bidding documents.

Application for Payment Contractor's written request for payment for completed portions of the work and, for materials delivered or stored and properly labeled for the respective project.

Architect One who designs and supervises the construction of buildings or other structures.

Architects Basic Services A recognized series of phases performed by an architect as follows: 1st Schematic Design Phase, 2nd Design Development Phase, 3rd Construction Document Phase, 4th Bidding or Negotiated Phase, 5th Construction Phase.

Architect-Engineer An individual or firm offering professional services as both architect and engineer.

Architectural Drawing A line drawing showing plan and/or elevation views of the proposed building for the purpose of showing the overall appearance of the building.

As-Built Drawings (also known as Record Drawings) Contract drawings marked up to reflect changes made during the construction process. It is good practice to make *As-Built drawings* by marking the changes on reproducible drawings such sepias for duplication purposes later.

Bid (1) An offer or proposal of a price (2) The amount offered or proposed.

Bid Bond A written form of security executed by the bidder as principal and by a surety for the purpose of guaranteeing that the bidder will sign the contract, if awarded the contract, for the stated bid amount.

Bid Date/Time The due date and time set by the owner, architect or engineer for receiving bids.

Bid Form A standard written form furnished to all bidders for the purpose of obtaining the requested information and required signatures from the authorized bidding representatives.

Bid Opening The actual process of opening and tabulating bids submitted within the prescribed bid date/time and conforming to the bid procedures. A Bid Opening can be open (where the bidders are permitted to attend) or closed (where the bidders are not permitted to attend). (See Bid Date/Time)

Bid Price The stipulated sum stated in the bidder's bid.

Bidding Documents The published advertisement or written invitation to bid, instructions to bidders, the bid form and the proposed contract documents including any acknowledged addenda issued prior to receipt of bids.

Bidding Period The calendar period allowed from issuance of bidding requirements and contract documents to the prescribed bid date/time. (See Bid Date/Time)

Bidding Requirements The written minimum acceptable requirements set forth by the owner to the contractor during bidding process. The owner usually reserves the right to reject a bid if the Bidding Requirements are not met. (See Bidding Documents)

Bid Shopper A buyer or client who seeks to play one proposed supplier or subcontractor against the other for the purpose of reducing a purchase price.

Bid Tabulation A summary sheet listing all bid prices. (See Bid Form)

Bid Time (see Bid Date/Time)

Bond (see Bid Bond; Contract Bond; Contract Payment Bond; Contract Performance Bond; Labor and Material Payment Bond; Performance Bond; Subcontractor Bond; surety)

Bonding Company A properly licensed firm or corporation willing to execute a surety bond, or bonds, payable to the owner, securing the performance on a contract either in whole or in part; or securing payment for labor and materials.

Budget (Construction Budget) (1) An itemized summary of estimated or intended expenditures for a given period of time (2) The total sum of money allocated for a specific project.

Building (1) To form by combining materials or parts (2) A structure enclosed within a roof and within exterior walls housing, shelter, enclosure and support of individuals, animals, or real property of any kind.

Building Code The legal requirements set up by the prevailing various governing agencies covering the minimum acceptable requirements for all types of construction. (See Codes)

Building Envelope (Sometimes referred to as Building Shell) (1) The waterproof elements of a building, which enclose conditioned spaces through which thermal energy may be transferred to or from the exterior. (2) The outer structure of the building. (See Tenant and Leasehold improvements for building interiors)

Building Inspector/Official A qualified government representative authorized to inspect construction for compliance with applicable building codes, regulations and ordinances. Courts have ruled that building inspections are exempt from errors and omissions liabilities.

Building Permit A written document issued by the appropriate governmental authority permitting construction to begin on a specific project in accordance with drawings and specifications approved by the governmental authority.

Building Process A term used to express every step of a construction project from its conception to final acceptance and occupancy.

Change Order A written document between the owner and the contractor signed by the owner and the contractor authorizing a change in the work or an adjustment in the contract sum or the contract time. A change order may be signed by the architect or engineer, provided they have written authority from the owner for such procedure and that a copy of such written authority is furnished to the contractor upon request. The contract sum and the contract time may be changed only by change order. A change order may be in the form of additional compensation or time; or less compensation or time known as a Deduction (from the contract) the amount deducted from the contract sum by change order.

Change Order Proposal (See Change Order) A change order proposal is the written document before it has been approved and affected by the Contractor and Owner. A change order proposal can be issued by either the contractor or the owner. The change order proposal becomes a change order only after it has been approved and affected by the Contractor and Owner.

Change Order Request A written document issued by the owner requesting an adjustment to the contract sum or an extension of the contract time; generally issued by the architect or owner's representative.

COD means "cash on delivery" which means that the contractor or vendor expects payment for the item when it is delivered and accepted.

Codes Prevailing regulations, ordinances or statutory requirements set forth by governmental agencies associated with building construction practices and owner occupancy, adopted and administered for the protection of public health, life safety and welfare. (See Building Code)

Construct To assemble and combine construction materials and methods to make a structure.

Construction The act or process of constructing.

Construction Cost (1) The direct contractor costs for labor, material, equipment, and services; contractor's overhead and profit; and other direct construction costs. Construction cost does not include the compensation paid to the architect, engineer and consultants, the cost of the land, rights-of-way or other costs which are defined in the contract documents as being the responsibility of the owner. (See Soft Costs)

Construction Documents A term used to represent all drawings, specifications, addenda, and other pertinent construction information associated with the construction of a specific project.

Construction Documents Phase The third phase of the architect's basic services wherein the architect prepares working drawings, specifications and bidding information. Depending on the architect's scope of services the architect may assists the owner in the preparation of bidding forms, the conditions of the contract and the form of agreement between the owner and contractor.

Construction Document Review The owners review of the borrower's construction documents (plans and specifications), list of materials, and cost breakdowns for the purpose of confirming that these documents and estimates are feasible and are in accordance with the proposed loan or project appraisal.

Construction Inspector (see Project Representative)

Construction Management Organizing and directing men, materials, and equipment to accomplish the purpose of the designer.

Construction Management Contract A written agreement wherein responsibilities for coordination and accomplishment of overall project planning, design and construction are given to a construction management firm. The building team generally consists of the owner, contractor and designer or architect.

Construction Phase The fifth and final phase of the architect's basics services, which includes the architect's general administration of the construction contract(s).

Consultant One hired by the owner or client to give professional advice.

Cost Breakdown (see Schedule of Values)

Cost Codes A numbering system given to specific kinds of work for the purpose of organizing the cost control process of a specific project.

Cost of Work All costs incurred by the contractor in the proper performance of the work required by the plans and specifications for a specific project.

Cost Plus Contract (see Cost Plus Fee Agreement)

Cost Plus Fee Agreement (Cost-Plus) A written agreement with the owner under which the contractor or the architect and engineer is reimbursed for his/her direct and indirect costs and, in addition, is paid a fee for his/her services. The fee is usually stated as a stipulated sum or as a percentage of cost.

Contract (1) An agreement between two or more parties, especially one that is written and enforceable by law (2) The writing or document containing such an agreement.

Contract Administration The contractual duties and responsibilities of the architect and engineer during the construction phase of a specific project.

Contract Bond A written form of security from a surety company, on behalf of an acceptable prime or main contractor or subcontractor, guaranteeing complete execution of the contract and all supplemental agreements pertaining thereto and for the payment of all legal debts pertaining to the construction of the project.

Contract Date (see Date of Agreement)

Contract Documents A term used to represent all executed agreements between the owner and contractor; any general, supplementary or other contract conditions; the drawings and specifications; all addenda issued prior to execution of the contract; and any other items specifically stipulated as being included in the contract documents.

Contract Over-run (Under-run) The difference between the original contract price and the final completed cost including all adjustments by approved change order.

Contract Payment Bond A written form of security from a surety company to the owner, on behalf of an acceptable prime or main contractor or subcontractor, guaranteeing payment to all persons providing labor, materials, equipment, or services in accordance with the contract.

Contract Performance Bond A written form of security from a surety company to the owner, on behalf of an acceptable prime or main contractor or subcontractor, guaranteeing the completion of the work in accordance with the terms of the contract.

Contract Period The elapsed number of working days or calendar days from the specified date of commencing work to the specified date of completion, as specified in the contract.

Contract Sum The total agreeable amount payable by the owner to the contractor for the performance of the work under the contract documents. (See Change Order)

Contract Time The time period set forth established in the contract documents for completing a specific project; usually stated in working days or calendar days. The contract time can only be adjusted by valid time extensions through change order.

Contractual Liability The liability assumed by a party under a contract.

Contractor A properly licensed individual of company that agrees to furnish labor, materials, equipment and associated services to perform the work as specified for a specified price.

Contractor's Option A written provision in the contract documents giving the contractor the option of selecting certain specified materials, methods or systems without changing in the contract sum.

Contractor's Qualification Statement A written statement of the Contractor's experience and qualifications submitted to the Owner during the contractor selection process. The American Institute of Architects publishes a standard Contractor's Qualification Statement form for this purpose.

Contracting Officer An official representative of the owner with specific authority to act in his behalf in connection with a specific project.

Critical Path The set of activities that must be completed on time for the project completion date to be met. Activities on the critical path have no slack time.

Critical Path Method (C.P.M.) A planning scheduling and control line and symbol diagram drawn to show the respective tasks and activities involved in constructing a specific project.

CSI Construction Specification Institute

CSI Master Format The CSI Master Format is a system of numbers and titles for organizing construction information into a regular, standard order or sequence. By establishing a master list of titles and numbers Master Format promotes standardization and thereby facilitates the retrieval of information and improves construction communication. It provides a uniform system for organizing information in project manuals, for organizing project cost data, and for filing product information and other technical data.

Currant Date Line A vertical line on the chart indicating the current date.

Daily Construction Report A written document and record that has two main purposes: (1) they furnish information to off-site persons who need and have a right to know important details of events as they occur daily and hourly, and (2) they furnish historical documentation that might later have a legal bearing in cases of disputes. Daily reports should be as factual and impersonal as possible, free from the expression of personal opinions and feelings. Each report should be numbered to correspond with the working days established on the progress schedule. In the event of no-work days, a daily report should still be made, stating "no work today" (due to rain, strike, or other causes). The report includes a description of the weather; a record of the total number of employees, subcontractors by name, work started and completed today, equipment on the job site, job progress today, names and titles of visitors, accidents and/or safety meetings, and a remarks column for other job related information.

Date of Agreement (1) Usually on the front page of the agreement (2) If not on front page it may be the date opposite the signatures when the agreement was actually signed (3) or when it was recorded (4) or the date the agreement was actually awarded to the contractor.

Date of Commencement of the Work The date established in a written notice to proceed from the owner to the contractor.

Date of Substantial Completion The date certified by the architect when the work or a designated portion thereof is sufficiently complete, in accordance with the contract documents, so the owner may occupy the work or designated portion thereof for the use for which it is intended.

Demising Walls The boundaries that separate your space from your neighbors' and from the public corridor.

Design A graphical representation consisting of plan views, interior and exterior elevations, sections, and other drawings and details to depict the goal or purpose for a building or other structure.

Design-Build Construction When a Prime or Main contractor bids or negotiates to provide Design and Construction services for the entire construction project.

Design-Construct Contract A written agreement between and contractor and owner wherein the contractor agrees to provide both design and construction services.

Design-Development Phase The second phase of the architect's basic services wherein the architect prepares drawings and other presentation documents to fix and describe the size and character of the entire project as to architectural, structural, mechanical and electrical systems, materials and other essentials as may be appropriate; and prepares a statement of probable construction cost.

Detail (1) An individual part or item (2) A graphical scale representation (drawing at a larger scale) of construction part(s) or item(s) showing materials, composition and dimensions.

Direct Cost (or expense) All items of expense directly incurred by or attributable to a specific project, assignment or task. Direct Costs, Hard Costs, and Construction Costs are synonymous. (See Construction Costs and Hard Costs)

Drawings (1) A term used to represent that portion of the contract documents that graphically illustrates the design, location and dimensions of the components and elements contained in a specific project (2) A line drawing.

Duration The length of an activity, excluding holidays and other non-working days.

Engineer (see Professional Engineer)

Estimate (1) To calculate approximately the amount, extent or value of something (2) To form an opinion of estimated costs.

Estimate of Construction Cost, Detailed A calculation of costs prepared on the basis of a detailed analysis of materials and labor for all items of work, as contrasted with an estimate based on current area, volume or similar unit costs.

Estimating A process of calculating the amount of material, labor and equipment required for a given project necessary to complete the work as specified.

Fast Track Construction (Fast Tracking) A method of construction management, which involves a continuous design-construction operation. When a prime or main contractor starts the construction work BEFORE the plans and specifications are complete. (See Design-Build Construction)

Field Order A written order effecting a minor change or clarification in the work not involving an adjustment to the contract sum or an extension of the contract time.

Field Report (see Daily Construction Report)

Field Work Order A written request to a subcontractor or vendor, usually from the general or main contractor, site for services or materials.

Final Acceptance The action of the owner accepting the work from the contractor when the owner deems the work completed is in accordance with the contract requirements. Final acceptance is confirmed by the owner when making the final payment to the contractor.

Final Inspection A final site review of the project by the contractor, owner or owner's authorized representative prior to issuing the final certificate for payment.

Final Payment The last payment from the owner to the contractor of the entire unpaid balance of the contract sum as adjusted by any approved change orders. (See Final Acceptance)

Finish Date The date that an activity or project is completed.

Fixed Fee A set contract amount for all labor, materials, equipment and services; and contractors overhead and profit for all work being performed for a specific scope of work.

Fixed Limit of Construction Costs A construction cost ceiling agreed to between the owner and architect or engineer for designing a specific project. (See Budget)

FF&E (1) An abbreviation for furniture, fixtures and equipment (2) Items classified as personal property rather than real property (3) An abbreviation generally associated with interior design and planning of retail stores or office facilities.

FOB This means "freight on board" which determines the place where the liability for the item(s) ends from the delivering party and begins with the receiving party.

Gantt chart The schedule of activities for a project. A Gantt chart shows start and finish dates, critical and non-critical activities, slack time, and predecessor relationships.

General Conditions (1) A written portion of the contract documents set forth by the owner stipulating the contractor's minimum acceptable performance requirements including the rights, responsibilities and relationships of the parties involved in the performance of the contract. General conditions are usually included in the book of specifications but are sometimes found in the architectural drawings. (2) General Conditions are sometimes confused with General Requirements. (See General Requirements).

General Contractor Properly licensed individual or company having primary (prime) responsibility for the work.

General Contracting (the traditional method) When a prime or main contractor bids the entire work AFTER the final design, plans and specifications are complete and have been approved by the owner. (See Design-Build Construction and Fast Track Construction)

General Requirements General Requirements (1) Are tasks, activities and functions usually hired or performed by the Prime or Main Contractor (2) These tasks, activities and functions involve cost and time thus making them important to include in the contract documents (3) General Requirements are sometimes confused with General Conditions. (See General Conditions)

Hard Costs (see Construction Costs and Direct Costs)

Independent Contractor One free from the influence, guidance, or control of another or others and does not owe a "fiduciary duty". Example: architect, engineer, prime or main contractor, construction manager at-risk.

Improvements (1) A term sometimes used to describe TI'S or Tenant Improvements. (2) Improvements can be in the form of new construction or remodel work. (See TI'S)

Indemnification (1) The act of indemnifying (2) The condition of being indemnified.

Indirect Cost (or expense) A contractor's or consultant's overhead expense; expenses indirectly incurred and not chargeable to a specific project or task. The terms indirect costs and soft costs are synonymous. (See Soft Costs)

Inspection (1) The act of inspecting (2) An official examination or review of the work completed or in progress to determine its compliance with contract requirements.

Inspection List (punch list) A list prepared by the owner or his/her authorized representative of items of work requiring immediate corrective or completion action by the contractor.

Inspection Report Sometimes used to describe an *Inspection List*. (See Inspection List)

Inspector One who is appointed or employed to inspect something.

Interior Finish A term used to represent the visible elements, materials and applications applied to a building's interior excluding furniture, fixtures and equipment. (See FF&E)

Invoice A list sent to a purchaser containing the items and charges of merchandise. (See Statement)

Labor and Material Payment Bond (1) A written form of security from a surety (bonding) company to the owner, on behalf of an acceptable prime or main contractor or subcontractor, guaranteeing payment to the owner in the event the contractor fails to pay for all labor, materials, equipment, or services in accordance with the contract. (See Performance Bond and Surety Bond)

Lead Time A term used in the bidding process usually associated with the delivery time of materials or equipment. Some items need to be fabricated or back ordered and occasionally items have shipping restrictions causing delays in receiving the item. This anticipated time delay is referred to as lead time. Lead time is usually calculated in days and included in the agreement and/or schedule.

Leasehold Improvements A term used to mean *Tenant Improvements*. Generally, this term is used when building in retail stores as contrasted with the term *Tenant Improvements* which are generally associated with office buildings. The terms are often used interchangeably. (See TI'S)

Lien, Mechanic's or Material The right to take and hold or sell an owner's property to satisfy unpaid debts to a qualified contractor for labor, materials, equipment or services to improve the property. (See Preliminary Lien Notice)

Lien Release A written document from the contractor to the owner that releases the Lien, Mechanic's or Material following its satisfaction.

Lien Waiver (1) A written document from a contractor, subcontractor, material supplier or other construction professional(s), having lien rights against an owner's property, relinquishes all or part of those rights. (2) Lien waivers are generally used for processing progress payments to prime or main or subcontractors as follows: Conditional Lien Waiver, Unconditional Lien Waiver, and Final Lien Waiver.

Lump Sum Agreement (See Stipulated Sum Agreement)

Lump Sum Bid A single entry amount to cover all labor, equipment, materials, services, and overhead and profit for completing the construction of a variety of unspecified items of work without the benefit of a cost breakdown.

Lump Sum Contract A written contract between the owner and contractor wherein the owner agrees the pay the contractor a specified sum of money for completing a scope of work consisting of a variety of unspecified items or work.

Meeting Attendance Form A form consisting of three columns (individuals name, individual's title, and company the individual represents). This form is given to all persons attending any meeting. Each person attending the meeting will fill in their respective information. The date of the meeting should be included for reference.

Meeting Notes A written report consisting of a project number, project name, meeting date and time, meeting place, meeting subject, a list of persons attending, and a list of actions taken and/or discussed during the meeting. Generally, this report is distributed to all persons attending the meeting and any other person having an interest in the meeting.

Milestone An activity with duration of zero (0) and by which progress of the project is measured. A milestone is an informational marker only; it does not affect scheduling.

Not to Exceed (sometimes referred to as Guaranteed Maximum Not to Exceed) A term used in the bidding process that means the cost will not exceed a specified amount to complete the work. Not to Exceed costs are subject to the terms and conditions of the construction documents and/or agreement. But as a rule when a contractor agrees to a "Not to Exceed" agreement the "Not to Exceed" amount is only exceeded for unforeseen conditions. (See Stipulated Sum Agreement)

Owner (1) An individual or corporation that owns a real property.

Owner-Architect Agreement A written form of contract between architect and client for professional architectural services.

Owner-Builder A term used to describe an Owner who takes on the responsibilities of the general contractor to build a specific project.

Owner-Construction Agreement Contract between owner and contractor for a construction project.

Owner-Construction Management Agreement Contract between construction manager and client for professional services.

Performance Bond (1) A written form of security from a surety (bonding) company to the owner, on behalf of an acceptable prime or main contractor or subcontractor, guaranteeing payment to the owner in the event the contractor fails to perform all labor, materials, equipment, or services in accordance with the contract. (2) The surety companies generally reserve the right to have the original prime or main or subcontractor remedy any claims before paying on the bond or hiring other contractors. (See Labor and Material Payment Bond and Surety Bond)

Performance Specifications The written material containing the minimum acceptable standards and actions, as may be necessary to complete a project. Including the minimum acceptable quality standards and aesthetic values expected upon completion of the project.

PERT An abbreviation for Program Evaluating and Review Technique. (See Activity; Critical Path Method)

PERT Schedule A diagram that illustrates charts and reports a project estimated start and completion times; and work in progress.

Plan (1) A line drawing (by floor) representing the horizontal geometrical section of the walls of a building. The section (a horizontal plane) is taken at an elevation to include the relative positions of the walls, partitions, windows, doors, chimneys, columns, pilasters, etc. (2) A plan can be thought of as cutting a horizontal section through a building at an eye level elevation.

Plan Checker A term sometimes used to describe a building department official who examines the building permit documents.

Planner A person who forms a scheme or method for doing something; an arrangement of means or steps for the attainment of some object; a scheme, method, design; a mode of action.

Plans A term used to represent all drawings including sections and details; and any supplemental drawings for complete execution of a specific project.

Pre-Construction Planning and Team Building A process used for the purpose of establishing below market dollar budget(s), overall project scheduling and design criteria; also identification and selection of the most feasible planning, design and construction team.

Predecessor An activity that must be completed before another activity can begin.

Preliminary Drawings The drawings that precede the final approved drawings. (2) Usually these drawings are stamped or titled "PRELIMINARY"; and the "PRELIMINARY" is removed from the drawings upon being reviewed and approved by the owner.

Preliminary 20-Day Notice (See Preliminary Lien Notice)

Preliminary Lien Notice A written notice given to the property owner of a specific project by the subcontractors and any person or company furnishing services, equipment or materials to that project. The notice states if bills are not paid in full for the labor, services, equipment, or materials furnished or to be furnished, a mechanic's lien leading to the loss, through court foreclosure proceedings, of all or part of the property being so improved may be placed against the property even through the owner has paid the prime contractor in full. The notice explains how the owner can protect himself against this consequence by (1) requiring the prime contractor to furnish a signed release by the person or firm thus giving the owner notice before making payment to the prime contractor or (2) any other method or device which is appropriate under the circumstances. The state of California mandates that a *Preliminary Lien Notice* must be given to the property owner not more than 20 days after starting the work on the specific project.

Pre-qualification of prospective bidders A screening process wherein the owner or his/her appointed representative gathers background information from a contractor or construction professional for selection purposes. Qualifying considerations include competence, integrity, dependability, responsiveness, bonding rate, bonding capacity, work on hand, similar project experience, and other specific owner requirements.

Prime Contract A written contract directly between a prime or main contractor and subcontractor for work on a specific project.

Prime Contractor Any contractor having a contract directly with the owner. (2) Usually the main (general) contractor for a specific project.

Principal The leading participant of professional practice.

Professional Engineer One who is professionally engaged in a branch of engineering.

Program An ordered list of events to take place or procedures to be followed for a specific project.

Progress Payment A payment from the owner to the contractor determined by calculating the difference between the completed work and materials stored and a predetermined schedule of values or unit costs. (See Schedule of values; Unit Costs).

Progress Schedule A line diagram showing proposed and actual starting and completion times the respective project activities. (See Activity)

Project A word used to represent the overall scope of work being performed to complete a specific construction job.

Project Cost All costs for a specific project including costs for land, professionals, construction, furnishings, fixtures, equipment, financing and any other project related costs.

Project Directory A written list of all parties connected with a specific project. The list usually includes a classification or description of the party (i.e., Owner, Architect, Attorney, General Contractor, Civil Engineer, Structural Engineer, etc.); name, address, telephone, FAX numbers or E-mail address opposite their respective classifications or description. It is particularly important that the emergency or after hour telephone numbers are included. These numbers should be kept confidential if requested by the respective parties.

Project Manager A qualified individual or firm authorized by the owner to be responsible for coordinating time, equipment, money, tasks and people for all or specified portions of a specific project. (See Construction Manager)

Project Manual An organized book setting forth the bidding requirements, conditions of the contract and the technical work specifications for a specific project. (See Specifications)

Project Representative A qualified individual authorized by the owner to assist in the administration of a specific construction contract.

Project Site (see Site)

Proposal A written offer from a bidder to the owner, preferably on a prescribed proposal form, to perform the work and to furnish all labor, materials, equipment and/or services for the prices and terms quoted by the bidder. (See Bid)

Proposal Form (See Bid Form)

Purchase Order A written document from a buyer to a seller to purchase materials, services, equipment or supplies with acceptable purchase terms indicated.

Punch List (See Inspection List)

Qualified An individual or firm with a recognized degree, certificate, or professional standing; or who by extensive knowledge, training and experience, has successfully demonstrated his/her abilities to identify and solve or resolve problems associated with a specific subject matter or project type.

Record Drawings (See As-Built Drawings)

Release of Lien A written action properly executed by and individual or firm supplying labor, materials or professional services on a project which releases his mechanic's lien against the project property. (See Mechanic's Lien)

Reimbursable Expenses (or Costs) Amounts expended for or on account of the project, which in accordance with the terms of the appropriate agreement, are to be reimbursed by the owner.

Resident Architect An architect permanently assigned at a job site who supervises the construction work for the purpose of protecting the owner's interests during construction.

Resident Engineer (inspector) An individual permanently assigned at a job site for the purpose of representing the owner's interests during the construction phase. (See Owner's Inspector)

R.F.I. (1) An abbreviation for Request for Information (2) A written request from a contractor to the owner or architect for clarification or information about the contract documents following contract award.

RFP (1) An abbreviation for Request for Proposal (2) A written request from a property owner or owner's representative for a cost proposal. The RFP generally includes all the necessary information required and instructions for submitting a cost proposal for a specific project or improvement.

Roll Out A loose term used to describe the rapid succession (completion) of similar projects over a given time period.

Safety Report The Occupational Safety and Health Act of 1970 clearly states the common goal of safe and healthful working conditions. A Safety Report is prepared following a regularly scheduled project safety inspection of the specific project.

Schedule A plan for performing work or achieving an objective.

Schedule of Values A statement furnished by the contractor to the architect or engineer reflecting the portions of the contract sum allotted for the various parts of the work and used as the basis for reviewing the contractor's applications for progress payments.

Schematic A preliminary sketch or diagram representing the proposed intent of the designer.

Schematic Design Phase The first phase of the architect's basic services in which the architect consults with the owner to ascertain the requirements of the project and prepares schematic design studies consisting of drawings and other documents showing the scale and project components for the owner's approval.

Scheme (1) A chart, diagram, or an outline of a system being proposed (2) An orderly combination of related construction systems and components for a specific project or purpose.

Scope of Work A written range of view or action; outlook; hence, room for the exercise of faculties or function; capacity for achievement; all in connection with a designated project. (See Performance Specifications)

Slack Time The flexibility with non-critical jobs that allows their start dates to be adjusted without affecting the project completion date.

Site The place where a structure or group of structures was, or is to be located (a construction site).

Soft Costs Soft Costs are cost items in addition to the direct Construction Cost. Soft Costs generally include architectural and engineering, legal, permits and fees, financing fees, construction Interest and operating expenses, leasing and real estate commissions, advertising and promotion, and supervision. (See Construction Cost)

Specifications A detailed, exact statement of particulars, especially statements prescribing materials and methods; and quality of work for a specific project. The most common arrangement for specifications substantially parallels the CSI (Construction Specification Institute) format. (See CSI)

Special Conditions A section of the conditions of the contract, other than the General Conditions and Supplementary Conditions, which may be prepared for a particular project. Specific clauses setting forth conditions or requirements peculiar to the project under consideration, and covering work or materials involved in the proposal and estimate, but not satisfactorily covered by the General Conditions. (See General Conditions)

Standard Details A drawing or illustration sufficiently complete and detailed for use on other projects with minimum or no changes.

Standard Dimension A measurement unique to a specific manufactured item.

Standards of Professional Practice A listing of minimum acceptable ethical principles and practices adopted by qualified and recognized professional organizations to guide their members in the conduct of specific professional practice.

Start Date The date that an activity or project begins.

Statement A copy or summary of any account covering a stated period. (See Invoice)

Statute of Limitations The period of time in which legal action must be brought for an alleged damage or injury. The period commences with the discovery of the alleged damage or injury; or in construction industry cases with completion of the work or services performed. Legal advice should be obtained.

Stipulated Sum Agreement A written agreement in which a specific amount is set forth as the total payment for completing the contract. (See Lump Sum Contract)

Structural Design A term used to represent the proportioning of structural members to carry loads in a building structure.

Structural Systems (frames) The load bearing assembly of beams and columns on a foundation. The beams and columns are generally fabricated off site and assembled on site. Other systems such as non-load bearing walls, floors, ceilings and roofs are generally constructed within and on the structural system.

Structure (1) Something constructed (2) A building put together based on specific plans and specifications.

Sub An abbreviation for Subcontractor.

Subcontract A written form of agreement between the prime or main contractor and another contractor or supplier for the satisfactory performance of services or delivery or material as set forth in the plans and specifications for a specific project.

Subcontractor A qualified subordinate contractor to the prime or main contractor.

Subcontractor Bond A written document from a subcontractor given to the prime or main contractor by the subcontractor guaranteeing performance of his/her contract and payment of all labor, materials, equipment and service bills associated with the subcontract agreement.

Sublet To subcontract all or a portion of a contracted amount.

Substantial Completion (See Date of Substantial Completion)

Substitution A proposed replacement or alternate offered in lieu of and represented as being equivalent to a specified material or process.

Substructure The supporting part of a structure; the foundation.

Sub-subcontractor An individual or firm having a written contract with a subcontractor to perform a portion of the work.

Sub-surface Investigation (1) A term used to represent an examination of soil conditions below the ground. (2) Investigations include soil borings and geotechnical laboratory tests for structural design purposes.

Successor (1) One that succeeds another (2) A scheduled activity whose start depends on the completion of one or more predecessors.

Superstructure The part of a building or other structure above the foundation.

Supervision (1) The act, process, or function of supervising construction materials, methods and processes for a specific project (2) Hands on field direction of the contracted work by a qualified individual of the contractor.

Supplemental Conditions (See Supplementary Conditions)

Supplementary Conditions A written section of the contract documents supplementing and qualifying or modifying the contracts general conditions. (See Conditions of the Contract)

Supplier An individual or firm who supplies and/or fabricates materials or equipment for a specific portion of a construction project but does not perform any labor on the project. (See Vendor)

Surety (see Bonding Company)

T&M (1) An abbreviation for a contracting method called Time and Materials (2) A written agreement between the owner and the contractor wherein payment is based on the contractor's actual cost for labor, equipment, materials, and services plus a fixed add-on amount to cover the contractor's overhead and profit.

Tenant's Rentable Square Feet Usable square feet plus a percentage (the core factor) of the common areas on the floor, including hallways, bathrooms and telephone closets, and some main lobbies. Rentable square footage is the number on which a tenant's rent is usually based.

Tenant's Usable Square Feet The square footage contained within the demising walls. (See Demising Walls)

TI'S (Tenant Improvements) TI'S is a term used to define the interior improvements of the project after the Building Envelope is complete. TI'S usually include finish floor coverings; ceilings; partitions; doors, frames, hardware; fire protection; HVAC consisting of branch distribution duct work, control boxes, and registers; electrical consisting of lighting, switches, power outlets, phone/data outlets, exit and energy lighting; window coverings; general conditions; and the general contractor's fee. The cost of tenant improvements are generally born by the tenant and the costs of tenant improvements will vary with every building, and with tenant requirements. (See Work Letter)

Time and Materials A loose term used to describe a contracting method for work being performed. The intent is that only the actual time spent and materials supplied and installed will be included in the final costs for completing the work as substantiated with time cards and receipts. It is not uncommon to include a Not to Exceed amount when entering into a Time and Materials arrangement. (See Not to Exceed)

Time (as time of the essence associated with a construction contract) A provision in a construction contract by the owner that punctual completion within the time limits or periods in the contract is a vital part of the contract performance and that failure to perform on time is a breach and the injured party is entitled to damages in the amount of loss sustained.

Time-and-a-half A term meaning any individuals normal billing hourly rate is increased by a multiple of 1.5 following predetermined normal working hours.

Timely Completion Completing the work of the contract before the date required.

Time of Completion The date or number of calendar or working days stated in the contract to substantially complete the work for a specific project. (See Date of Substantial Completion)

Transmittal A written document used to identify information being sent to a receiving party. The transmittal is usually the cover sheet for the information being sent and includes the name, telephone/FAX number, e-mail address and address of the sending and receiving parties. The sender may include a message or instructions in the transmittal. It is also important to include the names of other parties the information is being sent to on the transmittal form.

Travel Time Wages paid to workmen under certain union contracts and under certain job conditions for the time spent in traveling from their place of residence to and from the job.

Underwriters Laboratories Label (UL) A label on a product or manufactured item showing the material is regularly tested by, and complies with the minimum standards of the Underwriter's Laboratories specification for safety and quality.

U.B.C. (Uniform Building Code) The Uniform Building Code is one of the families of codes and related publications published by the International Conference of Building Officials (ICBO) and other organizations, such as the International Association of Plumbing and Mechanical Officials (IAPMO) and the National Fire Protection Association (NFPA), which have similar goals as far as code publications are concerned. The Uniform Building Code is designed to be compatible with these other codes, as together they make up the enforcement tools of a jurisdiction.

Uniform System (See CSI Format)

Unit Price Contract A written contract wherein the owner agrees to pay the contractor a specified amount of money for each unit of work successfully completed as set forth in the contract.

Unit Prices A predetermined price for a measurement or quantity of work to be performed within a specific contract. The designated unit price would include all labor materials, equipment or services associated with the measurement or quantity established.

Verbal Quotation A written document used by the contractor to receive a subcontract or material cost proposal over the telephone prior to the subcontractor or supplier sending their written proposal via mail, e-mail or facsimile.

Vendor One that sells materials or equipment not fabricated to a special design.

Work The successful performance of the entire scope of the project being performed for a specific construction project including labor, materials, equipment, and other associated items necessary to fulfill all obligations under the contract.

Working Drawing A drawing sufficiently complete with plan and section views, dimensions, details, and notes so that whatever is shown can be constructed and/or replicated without instructions but subject to clarifications. (See Drawings)

Work Order A written order, signed by the owner or his representative, of a contractual status requiring performance by the contractor without negotiation of any sort.

Work Letter A written statement (often called Exhibit B to a lease or rental agreement) of the specific materials and quantities the owner will provide at his own expense. The work letter defines the building standards, including the type of ceiling, the type and number of light fixtures, the size and construction of the suite-entry and interior doors. Building standards define the quality of tenant spaces. Generally, a Work Letter is associated with the leasing or renting of office space by a tenant within a Building Envelope. (See TI'S and Building Envelope)

Zoning Restrictions of areas or regions of land within specific geographical areas based on permitted building size, character, and uses as established by governing urban authorities.

Zoning Permit A document issued by a governing urban authority permitting land to be used for a specific purpose.

SUSHI

Sushi is a favorite food throughout the world. This section of the book covers almost everything you want to know about sushi and sushi making. It includes the origins of sushi and presents simple, easy, and healthy ways of preparing sushi.

Most importantly, this section is not intended for the reader to learn professional sushi making because sushi chefs undergo extensive training and learning to develop their special professional culinary skills. The methods, techniques and recipes covered in this section have been learned, refined and simplified by Taemi Westernoff. She has extensive experience in Japanese cooking and hopes to share this knowledge with others.

This Sushi section includes four parts:

Planning Sushi
Preparation
Plating
Chop Sticks Manners

There are probably hundreds of kinds of sushi because sushi receipts can be found throughout Japan using local ingredients and preparation methods. For example, Sushi recipes in Japan usually include fish and shellfish for ingredients and overall appearance, but because rice is the most essential part of sushi making anyone can find and use local ingredients to make beautiful and healthy sushi.

To simplify and better understand these many kinds of sushi (pronounced with a "Z" and spelled Zushi) the following preparation methods are featured:

1. **Chirashi Zushi (Mixed Rice Sushi)** which is made by mixing sushi rice with your favorite ingredients;

2. **Nigiri Zushi (Rice Ball Sushi)** which is made by molding bite size amounts of sushi rice into round or oblong balls and then pressing your favorite ingredients on top or around the rice ball;

3. **Maki Zushi (Rolled Rice Sushi)** which is made by placing your favorite ingredients on a layer of sushi on a square piece of dry roasted seaweed and then rolled. The roll is sliced into bite size pieces. Maki Zushi is sometimes referred to as a Seaweed Roll;

4. **Inari Zushi (Stuffed Fried Bean Curd Sushi)** which is made by stuffing hand molded rice balls into pockets of fried seasoned bean curd; and

5. **Oshi Zushi (Pressed Rice Sushi)** which is made by pressing layer(s) of sushi rice and your favorite ingredients together.

Brief History of Sushi

Rice as a Preservative
It is said that sushi originated in Southeastern Asia about 400 BC. Raw, cleaned and salted fish was preserved in naturally fermented rice. After a couple of months, the fish was removed from the rice. People ate the fermented fish but discarded the rice because the fermenting process, undoubtedly, produced a sour taste. Thus, Sushi (Zushi) was a term used to describe a sour taste. It appears that Sushi was a method used for preserving food rather than a type of food.

Sushi in Japan
Hundreds of year's later people in Japan mixed vinegar with rice and combined the rice mixture with local regional and seasonal ingredients. This is one of the reasons so many different types of sushi exist today. Each region in Japan preserves their own unique taste and preparation method(s) by using local ingredients and techniques which have been passed on for generations.

Early Sushi of Today
Some of the most familiar sushi of today originated in Edo (now Tokyo), in the early 1800's (believed to be 1822-1823). Edo's food service at that time mostly consisted of mobile food stalls. The most common ingredients used were tasty seaweed, fresh seasonal fish and shell fish from Edo bay. This sushi was called Edomae-Sushi, which means "in front of Edo bay". The best fish and shellfish were served as toppings on hand formed rice clumps called Haya-Sushi, which means "Speedy Sushi", and perhaps one of the first fast foods in Japan.

Sushi of Today
Nigiri-Sushi (Rice Ball Sushi) is probably one of the most popular outside of the Japan today. It was created and prepared by skilled Edomae-Sushi chefs around 1910 using sushi rice balls (rice clumps) with raw toppings marinated with vinegar and salt, and sometimes simmering or steaming the ingredients.

Sushi's Rise to Popularity

After the Kanto (near Edo now the Tokyo area) earthquake of 1923, skilled Edomae-Sushi chefs lost their jobs and moved from Edo to other areas in Japan for business. Because of these relocations they were able to spread their favorite sushi's' throughout Japan. In the 1980's sushi's popularity outside of Japan began mostly because of its well known healthy ingredients and people becoming more health conscious.

Author's Definition of Sushi

Sushi rice (Boiled rice mixed with rice vinegar, sugar, salt) beautifully mixed, topped, wrapped, or pressed with your favorite ingredient(s).

Planning Sushi

Chirashi Zushi (Mixed Rice Sushi)

Pictured is a mixture of sushi rice, mushrooms, carrots, boiled shrimp (sometimes chicken is used), and cut and boiled snap peas. To make the dish beautiful the mixture is topped with sliced eggs, and all ingredients. The carrots have been sliced a cut with a decorative culinary cutter in the shape of a flower.

Nigiri Zushi (Rice Ball Sushi)

The orange sushi pictured is seasoned fish Roe (fish eggs). A sushi rice ball is first wrapped with Nori (dry roasted seaweed) leaving a pocket at the top. The pocket is filled with the Roe. It's fun and noisy to eat - lots of crunchy popping going on!

Maki Zushi (Rolled Rice Sushi)

The roll pictured here has a blend of egg; the green is Japanese parsley, boiled shrimp, and dried radish. Avocado provides a surprisingly noticeable quality of richness to sushi. If you're hungry and a vegetarian, cucumber is a surprise. It's very refreshing and cool, and lends a nice crunch to the sushi.

Inari Zushi (Stuffed Fried Bean Curd Sushi)

This is seasoned fried bean curd stuffed will sushi rice. The fried bean curd is slightly sweet because it is prepared in a special seasoning. The seasoning requires a powered soup stock usually found in Japanese or Asian markets. Very tasty and healthy.

Oshi Zushi (Pressed Rice Sushi)

The pictured sandwich like pieces contain fish and vegetables pressed between top and bottom layers of sushi rice; and topped with fresh sliced mushrooms, boiled prawn, sashimi salmon, sliced cucumber; and even a piece of cheese. It's easy to make and beautiful to serve.

Most Common Sushi Ingredients

Short Grain White Rice

Dry Roasted Seaweed (Nori)

Season Fish and Shell Fish

Fresh Wasabi (Japan)

Prepared Wasabi

Soy Sauce

Sesame Seeds

Mushrooms

Pickled Radish

Fresh Crab (Dungeness)

Imitation Crab

Fresh Crab (Japan)

Fresh Fish Sausage (Japan)

Fish Sausage (Sautéed)

Fish Eggs (Roe)

Fresh Eggs

Fried Bean Curd (Age)

Renkon (Lotus Root)

Eel (Unagi) and Fried Egg

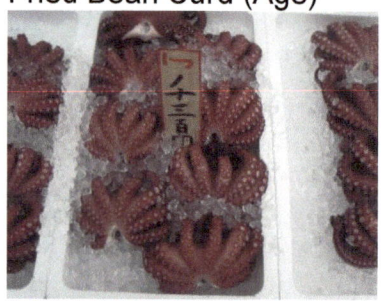
Octopus (Tako)

Avocado

Carrots (Sauteed or Fresh)

Bell Peppers

Spinach and Cucumber

Bamboo Shoots (Japan)

Steamed Bamboo Shoots

Gobo (Japan) Burdock Root

Fresh Pickles (Japan)

Seasoned Rice Vinegar

Rice Vinegar

Utensils for Making Sushi

Wooden bowl, spoon, fan

Glass Bowl (Optional)

Strainer in Bowl

Wooden or Plastic Spoon

Bamboo Roller Mat (Maki Su)

Chop Sticks on Rest

Plastic Rice Molds (Optional)

Plastic or Wood mold/Press for Oshi Zushi

Shark Skin Grater for fresh Wasabi (Japan). Use a metal or plastic grater.

PLANNING SUSHI

Date:
To:
From:
Preparation Address:

Here is a list of possible items or ingredients needed to make my next sushi dish:

ITEMS OR UTENSILES	YES	NO	MAYBE	NOTES
Automatic Rice Cooker	☐	☐	☐	
Pot for cooking rice	☐	☐	☐	
Strainer for draining the rice	☐	☐	☐	
Wooden or Plastic spoon for mixing and cooking the rice	☐	☐	☐	
Bamboo roller	☐	☐	☐	
Sushi molds	☐	☐	☐	
Sushi Press for Oshi Zushi	☐	☐	☐	
Cutting board	☐	☐	☐	
Sushi Knife	☐	☐	☐	
Chop Sticks	☐	☐	☐	
Bowl for Rice Preparation	☐	☐	☐	
Hand fan for cooling the rice	☐	☐	☐	

BASIC INGREDIENTS

	YES	NO	MAYBE	NOTES
White Rice Short Grain	☐	☐	☐	
Eggs	☐	☐	☐	
Fish Cake	☐	☐	☐	
Wasabi	☐	☐	☐	
Imitation crab meat	☐	☐	☐	
Fresh Cooked Crab	☐	☐	☐	
Avocado	☐	☐	☐	
Fish eggs	☐	☐	☐	
Cucumber	☐	☐	☐	
Radish	☐	☐	☐	
Sesame Seeds White	☐	☐	☐	
Sesame Seeds Black	☐	☐	☐	
Nori (Dry Roasted Seaweed)	☐	☐	☐	
Fried Bean Curd	☐	☐	☐	
Sushi Seasoning	☐	☐	☐	
Rice Vinegar	☐	☐	☐	
Pickles	☐	☐	☐	
Soy Sauce for dipping	☐	☐	☐	
	☐	☐	☐	

COMMON INGREDIENTS FOR CHIRASHI ZUSHI

Ingredient	YES	NO	MAYBE	NOTES
Bell Pepper (Red, green, yellow)	☐	☐	☐	
Carrots	☐	☐	☐	
Green beans	☐	☐	☐	
Snow peas	☐	☐	☐	
Gobo (Burdock Root)	☐	☐	☐	
Renkon (Lotus Root)	☐	☐	☐	
Mushrooms Fresh	☐	☐	☐	
Mushrooms Dry	☐	☐	☐	
Chicken	☐	☐	☐	
Shrimp	☐	☐	☐	
Eggs	☐	☐	☐	
Spinach	☐	☐	☐	
	☐	☐	☐	

COMMON INGRDIENTS FOR NIGIRI ZUSHI

Ingredient	YES	NO	MAYBE	NOTES
Sushi Rice balls	☐	☐	☐	
Prawns	☐	☐	☐	
Eel	☐	☐	☐	
Gizzard Shad	☐	☐	☐	
Squid	☐	☐	☐	
Fatty Tuna	☐	☐	☐	
Ark Shell	☐	☐	☐	
Octopus	☐	☐	☐	
Sea Beam	☐	☐	☐	
Salmon Roe	☐	☐	☐	
Tuna	☐	☐	☐	
Sea Urchin	☐	☐	☐	
Yellow Tail	☐	☐	☐	
	☐	☐	☐	
	☐	☐	☐	

COMMON INGRDIENTS FOR MAKI ZUSHI

Ingredient	YES	NO	MAYBE	NOTES
Sushi Rice	☐	☐	☐	
Nori (Dry Roasted Seaweed)	☐	☐	☐	
Avocado	☐	☐	☐	
Mayonnaise	☐	☐	☐	
Spinach	☐	☐	☐	
Fresh cooked crab	☐	☐	☐	
Imitation Crab Meat	☐	☐	☐	
Cucumber	☐	☐	☐	
Pan Fried Egg	☐	☐	☐	
	☐	☐	☐	

COMMON INGREDIENTS FOR INARI ZUSHI	YES	NO	MAYBE	NOTES
Sushi Rice	☐	☐	☐	
Fried Seasoned Bean Curd	☐	☐	☐	
Sesame Seed White	☐	☐	☐	
Sesame Seed Black	☐	☐	☐	
Soy Sauce for Dipping	☐	☐	☐	
	☐	☐	☐	
	☐	☐	☐	
	☐	☐	☐	

COMMON INGREDIENTS FOR OSHI ZUSHI	YES	NO	MAYBE	NOTES
Sushi Rice	☐	☐	☐	
See Suggested Ingredients for Oshi Zushi	☐	☐	☐	
	☐	☐	☐	
	☐	☐	☐	
	☐	☐	☐	

SUGGESTED INGREDIENTS FOR OSHI ZUSHI	YES	NO	MAYBE	NOTES
Sliced Red Bell Pepper	☐	☐	☐	
Slice Green Bell Pepper	☐	☐	☐	
Sliced Yellow Bell Pepper	☐	☐	☐	
Slice Mushrooms raw	☐	☐	☐	
Sliced cucumber	☐	☐	☐	
	☐	☐	☐	
	☐	☐	☐	

OTHER

	YES	NO	MAYBE	NOTES
Boiled Rice (No sushi seasoning)	☐	☐	☐	
Luncheon Meat	☐	☐	☐	
	☐	☐	☐	
	☐	☐	☐	
	☐	☐	☐	
	☐	☐	☐	
	☐	☐	☐	
	☐	☐	☐	
	☐	☐	☐	
	☐	☐	☐	
	☐	☐	☐	
	☐	☐	☐	
	☐	☐	☐	
	☐	☐	☐	
	☐	☐	☐	
	☐	☐	☐	
	☐	☐	☐	

Preparation

Boiled rice is the main ingredient for making sushi. The author prefers boiling rice the traditional way for making sushi rice. The illustrations in this section use the traditional method and tips for making perfect sushi rice. If you decide to use an automatic rice cooker follow your rice cooker instructions because all rice cookers have their own cooking instructions.

Tip!
For illustration purposes many of the photographs in this section are taken without wearing culinary gloves. It is strongly recommended that you wear gloves for safe food handling.

Rice

Rice is one of the main ingredients for making sushi rice, but there are many types and qualities of rice.

Selecting the Kind of Rice

There are many kinds of rice and rice in grown in almost all parts of the world and to complicate the selection further the grains of rice can be short, medium, or long. Japanese rice can generally be classified in two groups. They are Mochi rice (sometimes referred to as sticky rice) and basic Japanese rice.

The following table shows a partial list of rice types and descriptions found in your typical market or grocery store. Most of them are not recommended for making sushi:

Common Rice Types and Descriptions

Types of Rice			Descriptions
Brown Jasmine Rice	Japanese Rice	Jasmine Rice	**Short Grain (For Sushi)**
Premium Brown Rice	Multi Grain Rice	California Rice	Medium Grain
California Premium Rice	Brown Rice	Sweet Rice	Long Grain
White Rice (For Sushi)	Sweet Brown Rice		

Tip!
The brand or origin of rice is not as important as the freshness of the rice. If possible (because these dates are not always shown) find the "polishing date" or "best used before date" of the rice on the package. This insures that you are getting the freshest rice.

Tip!
Short Grain White Rice is recommended for making sushi rice.

The following table shows the amount of water, rice for each method featured in this section of the book. Also, the approximate serving sizes for each method.

Rice, Water and Servings

Rice	Water	Chirashi Zushi	Nigiri Zushi	Maki Zushi	Inari Zushi (See Tip below)	Oshi Zushi
1 Cup	1 Cup	Serves 2	6 medium	2 Rolls	8 Halves	2 medium
2 Cups	2 Cups	Serves 4	12 medium	4 Rolls	16 Halves	4 me(dium
3 Cups	3 Cups	Serves 6	18 medium	6 Rolls	24 Halves	6 medium
4 Cups	4 Cups	Serves 8	24 medium	8 Rolls	36 Halves	8 medium

Tip!
The bean curd for making Inari Zushi is usually cut into two halves. *(See Making Inari Zushi)*

Washing the Rice

Put the rice into a metal or plastic strainer and place the strainer inside of a bowl of water. Run water over the rice while stirring the rice with your fingers and/or the palms of your hands.

Wash the rice until the water drains clear or almost clear (usually three washings will make the water clear). Washing removes any starch, cleans the rice and makes it moist.

Tip!
Wash the rice quickly by pushing the grains of rice together using the heel and palm of your hands. This helps to prevent the bran (fiber) in the water from being absorbed by the rice.

Draining the Rice

Put the rice into a metal or plastic strainer to remove any excess water.

Tip!
Drain the rice for about thirty to sixty minutes. Thirty minutes during the summer or warmer seasons and sixty minutes for colder seasons.

Tip!
Prepare your ingredients while the rice is draining.

Cooking (Boiling) the Rice

Transfer the drained rice into a pot with one cup of cold water for each cup of rice and cover the pot. Cook the rice with high heat until the water begins to boil and the pot led begins to rattle (usually about five minutes for two cups of rice). Then immediately reduce the heat to low and cook for an additional ten minutes. _After cooking the rice for ten minutes turn the heat up to high and slowly count to ten._ After counting to ten remove the pot from the heat and let it stand covered for ten minutes. Remove the led and stir the rice.

Tip!
"After cooking the rice for ten minutes turn the heat up to high and slowly count to ten before removing the covered pan from the heat". This helps to remove excess moisture from the rice and inside the pot.

Making Sushi Rice

Sushi rice is made by adding a vinegar mixture (sometimes referred to as sushi seasoning) containing rice vinegar, sugar and salt to boiled rice. Select the quantities of rice and water from the above table. Wash, drain and cook (Boil) the rice. Put the hot cooked rice into a mixing bowl. A wooden bowl is ideal but any type of bowl will produce good sushi rice.

Tip!
For making your own sushi seasoning combine 3 Tablespoons of rice vinegar, 2 ½ Tablespoons of sugar and ½ Teaspoon of salt using a small pot. Cook over low heat until the sugar and salt is dissolved. Remove the pot of sushi seasoning from the heat and let it stand for about five minutes. This is enough sushi seasoning for making 2 cups of sushi rice.

Tip!
For sweeter sushi rice add more sugar to the sushi seasoning to taste

Tip!
Sushi seasoning is produced and sold in most local grocery stores.

While the rice is still hot slowly add the sushi seasoning using a spoon in a slicing and/or folding motion. Use only enough sushi seasoning to coat the rice.

Slowly cool the seasoned rice by fanning and using a slicing motion with the spoon until the rice begins to look shiny.

From the following tables select your favorite ingredients or toppings. These tables do not show all ingredients used in making sushi but the most common and popular ingredients are shown.

Tip!
Seasonal vegetables and sea foods are used for making the best sushi. Not to mention your favorite ethnic ingredients.

Tip!
Don't be afraid of being creative when making your own sushi.

Chirashi Zushi

Common Chirashi Zushi Ingredients

What	How	Other
Rice	*See Cooking (Boiling) the rice)*	
Sushi Rice Seasoning	*See Making Sushi Rice*	
Bell Pepper	Open the pepper and remove the seeds. Cut into ¾ inch long sections and then slice the sections into ¼ inch long strips	Boil the strips until tender
Carrots	Cut into ¾ inch long sections and then slice the sections into ¼ inch strips	Boil or microwave the strips with olive oil and/or salt to taste
Green beans or snow peas	Remove the strings from the beans or peas	Raw or cooked
Renkon (Lotus Root)	Peel and slice into thin (approximately ¼ inch pieces)	Marinade the pieces in salt water for about ten minutes, rinse, and then boil in fresh water until tender.
Gobo (Burdock Root)	Peel and cut into ¾ inch long sections and then slice the sections into ¼ inch strips	Marinade the strips in salt water for about ten minutes, boil in water until tender.
Mushrooms	Slice into desired size strips	Raw or sautéed
Dry Mushrooms	Soak in water to soften and slice into desired size strips	Sautee
Chicken	Cut into desired pieces	Cooked and sliced
Shrimp	Peel and clean	Boil until pink
Eggs	Beat and scramble add salt to taste	Slice into ¼" strips
Bamboo Shoots	Peel and clean in cold water	Boil until tender, slice into bite size pieces or strips
Mixed vegetables	Frozen is easy and add ham for additional flavor.	Sautee with cubed or chopped ham because the ham is already salted and has little oil.

Preparing Chirashi Zushi

Place the warm sushi rice into a mixing bowl and begin adding the ingredients.

Using a spoon continue adding the ingredients one by one in a folding motion.

Place the mixture into your serving bowl and sprinkle the top with small amounts of all ingredients used in the sushi.

Tip!
Do not over stir the rice to prevent it from becoming mashed or sticky.

Tip!
To make special shapes of ingredients for Chirashi Zushi toppings use culinary cutters **(Left)** Sliced carrots are beautiful **(Right)**

Nigiri Zushi

Common Nigiri Zushi Toppings

Name of Toppings and (Japanese Name)		
Prawn (Ebi)	Fatty Tuna (Toro)	Salmon Roe (Ikura)
Eel (Unagi)	Tuna (Meguro)	Sea Urchin (Uni)
Gizzard Shad (Kohada)	Octopus (Taco)	Yellowtail (Hamachi)
Squid (Ika)	Sea Beam (Tai)	Scallops (Kaibashara)
Egg (Tamago)	Ark Shell (Akagai)	Sea Urchin (Uni)
All of the above are sliced thin (about ¼ inch thick) to cover the top of the sushi rice balls. These ingredients should be very fresh and can be raw, simmered or steamed.		

Preparing Nigiri Zushi

Use two (first and middle) fingers to form the sushi ball.

Completed sushi ball or clump.

Use an optional rice mold to form the sushi ball.

Removing the rice mold.

Rice balls from mold.

Spread wasabi on topping.

Place rice ball on topping.

Shape and gently press the topping onto the rice ball.

Repeat the previous steps with other toppings.

Tip!
When using wasabi as an ingredient spread it on the topping first and then place the sushi rice ball on top of the topping and wasabi.

Tip!

Sliced luncheon meat **(Left)** makes a great topping on clumps of **Boiled Rice** (without sushi seasoning). Brown the luncheon meat and add a thin layer of pan fried egg between the meat and rice before wrapping all ingredients with a thin piece of Nori **(Right)**.

Maki Zushi

Common Maki Zushi Ingredients

What	How
Sushi Rice	*See Cooking (Boiling) the Rice*
Sushi Rice Seasoning	*See Making Sushi Rice*
Nori (Dry roasted seaweed) usually packaged in 8 inch square sheets	Place on top of Bamboo Roller and position as shown in the illustrations below.
Avocado	Slice and place on top of the rice
Imitation crab	Break into small pieces and place on top of the rice or mix the crab with mayonnaise to taste and spread on top of the rice
Fresh cooked crab meat	Break into small pieces and place on top of the rice or mix the crab with mayonnaise to taste and spread on top of the rice
Mayonnaise	Optional as a mixture
Spinach	Cook to desired hardness, slice and place on top of rice
Cucumber	Peel and slice into ¼ inch square strips and place on top of rice
Pan fried Egg	Slice into ¼ inch Strips
Carrots	Peel and slice into ¼ inch square strips and place on rice.

Tip!
For carrots and other hard vegetables add salt to taste and microwave for about one minute.

Preparing Maki Zushi Ingredients

Pan fried Egg.

Gently turn egg into thirds.

Remove from pan.

Slice into ¼ inch Strips.

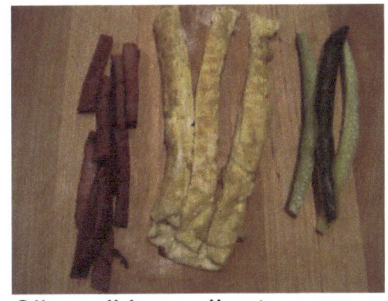
Slice all ingredients.

Ingredients ready for placing in sushi roll

Making Maki Zushi Rolls (Nori Outside)

Place a sheet of Nori directly on the bamboo roller. **Tip!** Place the shiny side of the Nori down. Also, Nori generally has lines going from side to side. Place the Nori so that the lines are parallel with the top and bottom of the Bamboo Roller.

Using your fingers apply a small amount of sushi seasoning to the Nori before placing the rice. You can also use the sushi seasoning to seal the edges while rolling the sushi.

Use approximately one cup of sushi rice to spread on the Nori.

Tip!
Keeping your hands wet helps prevent the rice from sticking to your hands when handling the rice.

Keep the upper edge of the Nori clear and make a valley for the ingredients with your finger.

Place your favorite ingredients into the valley area.

Begin rolling the sushi as shown.

Continue rolling while keeping the leading edge of the bamboo roller out.

Your almost finished roll with look like this

Place your roll to one edge of the bamboo roller.

Roll the bamboo roller around the sushi roll and press the end of the sushi to make a neat ends.

Repeat these two last steps for the other end of your sushi roll.

Tip!
Let the ingredients hang out of the ends of the sushi rolls before slicing the rolls. Makes a fun and interesting way of displaying the rolls at parties or special events before slicing them into bite size pieces.

Making Maki Zushi Rolls (Sushi Rice Outside)

Completely wrap a bamboo roll with plastic wrap. The plastic wrap is optional but helps prevent the rice from sticking to the bamboo roller.

Place a half sheet of Nori (shiny side down) on the bamboo roller. Use a full sheet of Nori if you like, but a half sheet is more managable.

Completely cover the Nori with sushi rice. Gently press the rice onto the Nori.

Sprinkle the rice with sesame seeds or any other seasoning of choice. This will be the outside of your sushi roll.

Gently lift the rice covered Nori; turn it over; and place it back on the bamboo roller as shown.

Place your favorite sushi ingredients as shown. Usually three ingredients fill the roll nicely.

Use the same rolling technique for making sushi with Nori outside above.

Place your roll to one edge of the bamboo roller.

Roll the bamboo roller around the sushi roll and press the end of the sushi to make a neat ends.

Combining three Nigiri Zushi Rolls into one Roll

Cover a half sheet Nori with sushi rice leaving the top and bottom edges of the Nori clear because when rolling the sushi the edges will be pinched and sealed. Make three sushi rolls with different color ingredients.

Make sushi rolls in a tear drop shape so that the ends are pinched together instead of rolled together as shown.

Place the three rolls on a full sheet of Nori on the bamboo roller. Roll the three rolls as shown and seal the end with a small amount of sushi seasoning

Continue rolling the completed roll by pulling the two sides of the bamboo roller up and down as shown. This will help make the roll perfectly round.

Your finished roll with three rolls inside with look like this. *See slicing Nigiri Zushi Rolls Below.*

Here is what your combined rolls look like after slicing and plating

Slicing Nigiri Zushi Rolls

Nigiri Zushi rolls ready for slicing.

Keep knife blade damp with wet paper towel or cloth before slicing.

Slice the roll into two equal pieces first.

Slice each half into two equal pieces.

Slice each remaning pieces into equal pieces (usually 1/2 inch thick pieces).

Use the same steps for this sushi roll.

Inari Zushi

Preparing Inari Zushi Age (Fried Bean Curd)

What	How
Fried Bean Curd (Age) Unseasoned	Usually available frozen containing five pieces per package. *(See Making Inari Zushi or the Tip on the bottom of the next page)*
Powdered Soup Stock. Many Japanese brands are available but usually made with dried Bonita, Shrimp or Kelp.	If in English follow the cooking instructions on the package or add 1 2/3 cups of water to one pouch and bring to boil, turn down to medium heat for ten minutes.
Fried Bean Curd Seasoning. This recipe is enough for seasoning ten halves of Fried Bean Curd. *(See Making Inari Zushi)*	Add the following ingredients to the cooked powered soup stock mixture above: 3 Tablespoons of Soy Sauce 5 Tablespoons of Sugar 1 Pinch of salt 3 Tablespoons of Sweet Cooking Sake (The cooking sake is optional for a sweeter seasoning) Cook on medium heat for thirty minutes *(See Making Inari Zushi below)*

Tip for eating Nigiri, Maki and Inari Zushi!

Pick up one piece of sushi using chop sticks or your fingers, dip into your favorite soy sauce mixture, and enjoy.

Tip!
Using your chop stick spread a small amount of wasabi directly on the top of the sushi for a greater wasabi taste.

Tip!
Mix wasabi with soy sauce in a small dish. Using chop sticks pick up a slice of pickled ginger and use the ginger as a brush to spread the wasabi soy mixture on top of your sushi because its much neater than dipping or soaking the sushi in the mixture.

Making Inari Zushi

Place the fried bean curd into a strainer and pour boiling water over it to remove the oil (a couple of drainings may be needed).

Cut the pieces in half. One package of five with yield ten Inari Zushis.

This photo shows all pieces cut in half and fried bean curd seasoning *(See Preparing Fried Bean Curd Seasoning above).*

Pour the fried bean curd seasoning into a pot containing the sliced fried bean curd.

Place a led inside the pot on top of the fried bean curd (a wooden drop lid is best) to press the bean curd while cooking.

Cover the pot and bring to a boil, turn down to low heat for thiry minutes. Remove form heat and let cool until used below.

Add your favorite ingredients to Sushi Rice or Rice only for stuffing. Gently fold the ingredients into the Sushi Rice..

Open one piece of the seasoned bean curd (the bean curd has an opening at one side) and gently stuff it with the sushi rice mixture and seal the end.

Turn the stuffed bean curd sushi over so that the sealed end is on the bottom and place the sushi on a serving plate.

Tip!
You can usually find the Inari Zushi Age (fried bean curd) already prepared (seasoned) in the frozen food section of you local Asian food store. Saves lots of time because you only need to stuff your Sushi Rice into the Age and serve.

Oshi Zushi

Making Oshi Zushi (using a plastic mold/press)

Place a bottom layer of sushi rice in the mold and gently press it smooth

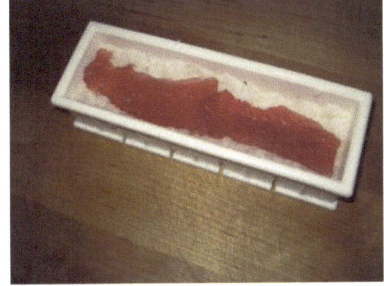

Add one layer of your favorite ingredient(s)

Add the top layer of rice in the mold

Level the rice in the mold.

Press the top of the mold firmly into the mold.

Remove the mold top.

Slice into equal size pieces.

Turn the mold over and remove the mold.

Separate the pieces, add your favorite topping(s), and place on a serving plate.

Making Oshi Zushi Salad

Gently press sushi rice into a small dish lined with plastic wrap (Leave enough wrap to fold over the top).

Fill the dish to top with the sushi rice.

Completely cover the rice by folding the plastic wrap over it.

Place a couple of unopened cans on top of the rice for about five minutes to press the rice.

Turn the dish and rice over and onto a board (by placing a plate on top and turning it over).

Remove the dish and plastic wrap from the rice.

Place a bed of your favorite vegetable on a serving plate (Fresh spinach shown)

Using a spatula lift and place the rice onto the bed of vegetables

Prepare a pan fried egg omelet. Season to taste.

Slice the omelet into small strips

Cover the rice with the egg strips

Add layers of your favorite topping ingredients.

Pictured toppings are boiled shrimp, pamento, sliced red bell peppers, and diced carrots.

Continue adding toppings. Pictured are sliced green beans and red bell peppers.

Oshi Zushi Salad ready for serving. Very easy and heathy.

Making Temaki Zushi (Simple hand wrapped sushi)

Place a small amount of sushi rice at a slight angle on one corner of a half sheet of Nori. Add your favorite ingredients.

Gently begin rolling the rice and ingredients into a cone shape.

Your finished roll will look like this.

Tip! Use very dry and fresh Nori for Temaki Sushi.

Tip!
Fill the Nori cone with Natto (Japanese fermented and seasoned soybeans). Usually found in most Asian stores.

Tip!
Mix a chopped green onion and a little Japanese mustard into the Natto before eating.

Making Hand Rolled Sushi

Left-Place sushi rice and your favorite ingredients on half of a half sheet of Nori.

Right-Roll the Nori and seal the edge with a small amount of sushi seasoning. Dip into soy sauce mixture and enjoy.

Plating

On a green leaf

Wooden board

Bamboo Leaf

Ceramic plate

Plastic Party Tray

Plastic Bento Box

Chop Sticks Manners

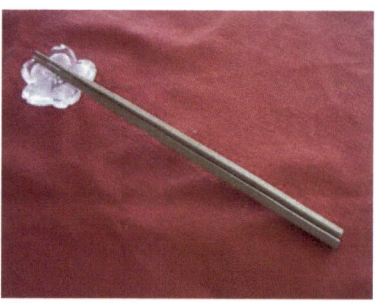

Chop stick rests are usually provided. If not, you can always fold the paper chopstick wrapper to use as a rest.

 Please don't spear food with your chop sticks

Please don't pull dishes with your chip sticks

Be deliberate when deciding on the food to pick up and eat.

Please don't move your chop sticks from item to item while deciding.

Please don't point your chop sticks at another person.

Please don't take or pass food from chop sticks to chop sticks.

Please don't examine the food on your plate with your chop sticks.

Please don't lick the tips of your chop sticks.

Please don't point your chop sticks at another person.

Bibliography

W. Gary Westernoff *Construction Management Made Easy.* Moraga: The Westernoff Group, 1998

Nipponia *Nipponia Discovering Japan*. No. 47, 2008 ISSN1343-1196. Tokyo: Heibonsha Ltd. 2008

The History of Sushi. http://sushi-master.com/usa/whatis/history.html

The worksheets in the **Construction** section of this book are being used with the permission of Ponta, Inc.

The photographs of the Mitsukan Seasoned Rice Vinegar and Rice Vinegar in the **Sushi** section of this book are being used with the permission of Mizkan Americas, Inc.

The "About the Author's" photograph was taken in Japan. The ceramic figures surrounding the authors are Tanuki statues also known as Raccoon Dogs. Raccoon Dogs are real animals found in Japan, but their statues can be seen throughout Japan in front of and/or inside homes and business establishments symbolic of welcome and good luck.

Another Westernoff Group publication you may find useful:

Construction Management Made Easy or do I really want to manage that Project Myself, by W. Gary Westernoff, ISBN 0-9668245-0-4

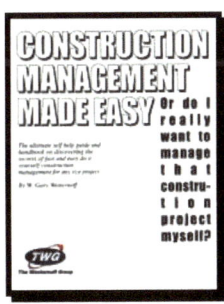

BULK SALES

The Westernoff Group publishing offers excellent discounts on their publications when ordered in quantity for bulk purchases or special sales. For more information contact The Westernoff Group.

www.ingramcontent.com/pod-product-compliance
Lightning Source LLC
Chambersburg PA
CBHW041545220426
43665CB00002B/36